CONTENTS:

Introduction:

Since the conception of this Country we have been gradually losing our freedom. Our Constitution has been distorted into something unrecognizable. If we don't do something to stop it soon we could lose it all! I hope I can give you some idea about what is happening and how we can hopefully change it. The rest will be up to you. This Once Great Nation is changing and as this Country changes so does the story, because Thee Great American Illusion is a never ending story.

Some Historic Background

I am a Former Elected Official in California, and I have seen the waste and self serving attitudes of public servants, and how the government treats the citizens. Most of the people have no idea how our government works or how it is really suppose to work. This is the reason I decided to write a book. I am going to show you some history and facts so you can get a better idea of what freedom we had and what freedom we lost, and how we can hopefully get some of it back or at least try to stop the total destruction, and keep what little freedom we have left.

I was told by a fellow politician that it is better to be the duper than the duped, and unfortunately that is exactly how many people in the government think. The sad reality is that most elected officials only care about their popularity status and go along to get along with the public servants or (serpents). I know a lot of people in elected office think they are the Duper, but in reality they are really the Duped because most of them are controlled and manipulated from the moment they get elected.

When I was in office, the city's police chief told me that elected officials come and go but the city staff will still be here long after. What he basically was telling me, was I wasn't going to change anything because it really was the staff and public employees that called the shots. I may not have really changed the waste and corruption I saw, but I gave them hell on the floor, and the local newspaper had me on the front cover more than any other local politician in the Yuba/Sutter areas history. They relentlessly tried to paint me as a trouble maker. When my term ended and I was planning to get out of California altogether; the paper even depicted me in a cartoon with a loaded truck saying; *"I'm outta here!"* No other local politician had ever been elevated to cartoon character in the opinions page... that was reserved for state and national politicians... But there I was.

Well, needless to say my outspokenness and refusal to give up on my belief in the Bill of Rights sold a lot of local daily newspapers. Their relentless attack on me to try and make me look bad was the reason I decided to start my own newspaper in 1997 called The Nor-Cal Paper. It was a weekly political paper that informed the citizens of the real truth that was going on in our local and state government; such as the corruption of a local Mayor who was investigated by the Yuba County Grand Jury because of the paper trail of illegal real estate activity that The Nor-Cal Paper had uncovered. This caused the mayor to resign. There was also a councilman who resigned because of evidence uncovered by The Nor-Cal paper against him of Abuse of Power. The local daily newspaper would never have reported or even investigated any of this news and didn't even say a thing until the Grand Jury report came out basically indicting the mayor. If it would have been me I would have been crucified, but the mayor was the local daily's fair-haired boy.

Sadly many local newspapers never report the real abuse of power committed by corrupt elected officials because they rely on the Legal Ads from the city and county and also because they are "Adjudicated" by the local court as a legally recognized newspaper, so they don't want to upset the powers that be. I think most of you have also noticed that a lot of newspapers and media create the news by omission and down right lies. Especially if they are supporting a politician and don't want negative news to get out to the voters, or they are trying to discredit a politician that they don't want in office. Consequently the local Yuba-Sutter daily newspaper eventually went bankrupt and was sold to another news group.

The City of Marysville is like so many other cities in California and across the nation that are getting close to the same fate "bankruptcy". Yet people across the nation still tend to believe the lies of the deceptive politicians and those media outlets with their own agendas, and they keep electing people who tell them what they want to hear and make grandiose promises. Then once they are elected they don't do what they promised and make things worse.

It has been over 20 years since I first stepped into the political arena as an elected official. I tried to tell people the truth about what is really going on in our government. I soon found out that most people do not want to hear it. They just want to hear the positive things that most of the politicians contrive... Unfortunately when you refuse to see and hear the negatives, there can never be any real positives; only a dreamy illusion that everything is coming up roses. If we keep looking through those rose colored glasses, and refuse to see the dark truth, things will eventually come crashing down and could turn into our darkest nightmare. Then it might be too late to do anything about it!

It is amazing to me that people do not seem to care about any of the wrong doings and down right corruption and out of control spending that is going on in our government. Most people just seem to ignore it and just put up with it. I can't understand why people are so complacent and apathetic? Maybe it's because they feel helpless and don't know what to do? Or maybe they just don't care about their freedom or the financial stability of our Country? So we keep allowing our elected leaders to spend way too much on salaries, Cadillac pensions and health insurance plans for public employees that normally only CEO executives of multi-million dollar corporations have. Because of this, there are many Cities on the edge of bankruptcy, and their States are following close behind if the elected leaders voted into office do not start conserving the Taxpayers money. The things that most of our politicians spew, such as giving up our freedom for security because it is better for America and the lie that it will not hurt our freedom, and everything is going to be just fine, is sadly what many of the people tend to believe and want to hear. This is why this once much freer Nation is headed for total enslavement.

Our Founding Fathers never intended Public Service to become a permanent get rich job at the taxpayer's expense. It was never intended that we should have to give up our freedom for the illusion of our security. Thank God not everyone wants to hear lies, and some of you are waking up. This is the real "positive" that is coming out of the negative situation America is in today.

I know that those of you who are starting to wake-up are seeing the same things I see. It is looking like our freedom and security will soon come to an end if this Country doesn't get back to its intended limited republic form of government. One of our founding fathers had foreseen the same thing 226 years ago. At the close of the Constitutional Convention on September 17, 1787, as Benjamin Franklin left the hall in Philadelphia, he was asked, *"What kind of government have you given us, Dr. Franklin?" He replied: "A republic, if you can keep it."* From what I can deduce by his statement, there must have been ranker and discord amongst those who wanted more of a Democratic Democracy and those who wanted a strong Democratic Republic.

What most people are not aware of is that there were independents like Franklin and Washington (though Washington leaned Federalist), Jefferson, and Madison (who helped write the Federalist Papers), who weren't part of a political party in the beginning, and then there were the Federalists, like Hamilton and Adams which believed in strong government powers. Both sides however saw the down-side to a Democratic Democracy and the rest is history.

John Adams who was a Federalist had said; *"Remember, democracy never lasts long. It soon wastes, exhausts, and murders itself. There never was a democracy yet that did not commit suicide."*

Article 4, Section 4 of the United States Constitution shall guarantee to every state in this union a republican form of government, and shall protect each of them against invasion; and on application of the legislature, or of the executive (when the legislature cannot be convened) against domestic violence. This meant all States would have the same

8

form of government and the Federal Government would protect them against invasion and attack. But Article 4, Section 4 was shredded when the north and federal government invaded the south.

James Madison, who has been called the Father of the Constitution had this to say; *"Hence it is that such democracies have ever been spectacles of turbulence and contention; have ever been found incompatible with personal security or the rights of property; and have in general been as short in their lives as they have been violent in their deaths... A republic, by which I mean a government in which the scheme of representation takes place, opens a different prospect and promises the cure for which we are seeking."*

The events and quotes are from documented facts and statements recorded down in time so they are as factual as anyone can get today or as factual as those who recorded history wanted people to believe. Because as many of you know; to the victor goes the spoils and how history is to be written. This book is filled with facts and figures that some of you may not know. – R.W. Gless

Chapter One

How Free Were We?

There was never any real freedom in America from its conception. There was only an idea written down in the Bill of Rights that granted free men inalienable rights, yet the chains of bondage were alive and well. Men, woman, and children of all races and colors were in servitude for a plethora of different reasons, and it was only going to get worse.

In the beginning of this country things were much more free than today. The people didn't have to worry about the dictates of a king or about paying half of everything they had to a controlling government. They didn't have to worry about over regulation of everything they owned and everything they did. Times may have been harder, but it was also a much simpler time, the people were able to adapt to survive and become self-sufficient. You either lived or died by your own toil and cunning, no one gave you a free ride. Today Americans resemble ants in a nest and bees in a hive, swarming around the government catering to their every need, like bees and ants swarm around their queen. I often wonder what our founding fathers would think if they could see how most of our Constitution has become null and void and how draconian our government has become. I am sure that they would not be happy with how it has all turned out.

The beginning of the Revolutionary War wasn't a total rebellion of all the people, most of the people living in the colonies were subservient to the King of England and liked it. What has not been taught in school is that only about 35% of the population was directly involved in fighting the King and his Red Coats. About 15% of them were comprised of wealthy colonists that were unhappy with what they saw as excessive taxation, that was arbitrary, and they were really the ones who started the rebellion. The Taxes back then were a lot like taxes we see today, but nowhere near to the excess we see today. Of the other 65% about half were Loyalists and the other half were what I like to call "Complacent" and "Apathetic", they would change suit to whatever side fit them at the time, a lot like Americans are today.

Most people today think the founding fathers and all of the patriots fought because they were being oppressed and over taxed by England, and for the most part they would be right; people also wanted control of their own lives and realized they did not need the British or any other government to survive. What a lot of people do not know is that a majority of those who fought against the British were actually mercenaries who expected to be paid, and were promised payment by the Continental Congress which was mostly made up of unhappy wealthy colonists. Now the problem was where was the money going to come from? The Articles of Confederation did not allow the newly formed government to tax. So the only idea they could come up with was one that was as old as warfare itself, Plunder. Plunder was what the buccaneers and privateers would take from the British, and for their service a percentage of the plunder they took was given to them and they were also given safe haven in ports controlled by the colonial army. The Privateers were very helpful when we needed ships and supplies, but later some of them went rogue which became very problematic. Privateers work for a side or government and fly that government flag, but some really started to like the plunder and decided to attack all ships and they became pirates.

The British on the other side also used privateers, Loyalist and Slaves. In 1775 at the start of what the Royal Governor Lord Dunmore of Virginia saw as a rebellion brewing issued a proclamation that promised freedom to servants and slaves of all color who were able to bear arms and join the Loyalist Regiments. The Regiment most talked about was his Loyalist Ethiopian Regiment. About 800 black slaves joined and they helped beat the Virginia militia at the Battle of Kemp's Landing. They also fought in the Battle of Great Bridge on the Elizabeth River, wearing the motto "Liberty to Slaves", which they lost. Black colonial slaves were often the first to come forward to volunteer and a total of 12,000 African Americans served with the British from 1775 to 1783. This forced the Patriot rebels to also offer freedom to those who would serve in the Continental Army, but sadly many of the promises were reneged upon by both sides. The British also had the largest fleet in the world at the time, and getting supplies from allies like France and Spain at the start of the war was a problem. France finally allied with American Colonies February 6, 1778 when Benjamin Franklin went to France and signed the Treaty of Amity and Commerce and the Treaty of Alliance. The Treaty of Amity and Commerce recognized the U.S. as an independent nation and promoted trade between France and America. The second agreement, the Treaty of Alliance, made the fledgling United States and France allies against Great Britain in the Revolutionary War. France decided to back the U.S. in its military efforts until the U.S. had full independence from Great Britain. After that, the treaty required France and the U.S. to work together on any peace agreement. Without the help from France the U.S. could not have won the Revolutionary War.

The Dutch, Spanish and South India Kingdom of Mysore ruled by the Wodeyar family also helped us during the war. They saw this as a way to weaken England, but not quite as openly as France did. Even with all the help we had, the war raged on and the Revolution was in jeopardy. Many of the troops demanded payment and were about to turn and march in on the Continental Congress. General George Washington was not about to let that happen, he stopped the troops from turning by executing their leaders and then told them that whoever spoke of treason again would meet the same fate. This was the beginning of intimidation by force and threat of death long before this country had won its independence.

After America finally won the war it needed to make good on the promise it made to pay those who help them defeat the British. The newly formed government had no money and needed to raise some fast before what they fought so hard for fell apart. The USA was deeply in debt, 79 million was owed in total. 54 million was owed by the Continental Congress and 25 million was owed by the states. The newly elected Secretary of Treasury Alexander Hamilton was a staunch Federalist and wanted to create a system that would give power to the Federal Government to control the States and place the government debt on the citizens. They needed a new set of laws to do that, so the Constitution was created and ratified replacing the Articles of Confederation that did not give the government power to tax the people. In 1789 the new Federal Government was created at the behest of Alexander Hamilton following the ratification of the United States Constitution. There was only one way they could come up with the money fast and that was Taxes! This was the very thing they opposed that the British had done, yet they were about to embark on the same path that would one day pale in comparison.

A National Democracy or a Republic?

From the beginning there were those who wanted a democracy which would have doomed America and our freedom much quicker, but the virtues of a Republican form of government prevailed and it was never totally accepted by the Federalists who believed in a stronger government controlled Democracy. The Federalists pushed for a national bank, tariffs, and good relations with Britain and came up with the Jay Treaty that was negotiated in 1794. Hamilton also developed the concept of implied powers, and successfully argued that his interpretation was in the United States Constitution. Their political opponents, the Republicans, led by Thomas Jefferson and James Madison, denounced most of the Federalist policies,

15

especially the National bank and implied powers, which gave the Federal Government a wider range of powers and they vehemently attacked the Jay Treaty as a sell-out of republican values to the British monarchy... Which is exactly what it was.

The Whiskey Tax

The Whiskey tax began in 1791, during the Presidency of George Washington. Farmers who used their leftover grain and corn to make whiskey to exchange for goods were forced to pay a new tax. The tax was a part of Treasury Secretary Alexander Hamilton's program to increase the Federal government's power, to fund the war debt by taxing the citizens of states which had failed to pay.

Whiskey Tax was not a popular tax at all, and the distillers resisted, many of whom were war veterans that had fought in the Revolutionary war, and were against taxation without local representation and affirmation. Of course the Federal Government maintained the taxes were legal under the taxation powers of Congress. But those against the Whiskey Tax saw this as a major betrayal of what they had fought for by the newly created government.

Protest arose and the people violently refused to pay. They used intimidation and threats of another revolution to prevent federal officials from collecting the tax. Resistance came to a head in July 1794, when a U.S. marshal arrived in western Pennsylvania to serve writs to whiskey distillers who had not paid the excise tax. The people were furious, and more than 500 armed men attacked the fortified home of tax inspector General John Neville.

FAMOUS WHISKEY INSURRECTION IN PENNSYLVANIA.

President Washington responded by sending peace commissioners to western Pennsylvania to negotiate with the rebels, while at the same time he called on state governors to send a militia army to enforce the excise tax which was later called a luxury tax. 13,000 militiamen were sent by the governors of Virginia, Maryland, New Jersey, and Pennsylvania, to put down the rebellion. President Washington rode at the head of the army to suppress those who would not comply and pay the tax. The stage was set for the new American Taxation that would bring down freedom by Federal government enforcement of any tax or law the Federal government deemed legal.

The Whiskey Rebellion also demonstrated to the people that the new national government had the willingness and ability to suppress violent resistance to its laws. The whiskey excise tax always remained difficult to collect. However the event contributed to the quick formation of another political party in the United States, a process that was already underway, but the oppression of the people by the Federalists made those against this oppression move much more quickly. So the newly created Republican Party, which was more like the Conservative Constitutionalist Libertarians of today, was formed by Thomas Jefferson, which opposed Hamilton's Federalist Party because the Federalist policies called for a national bank, tariffs, and they especially opposed any good relations with Britain. This was something Jefferson and Madison strongly disagreed with... After all we just fought a bloody war with the British and they despised the Constitution. The Republicans also believed that Policitical Parties were divisive and harmful to republicanism, but to combat the Federalists contrary to their beliefs, Jefferson's Republican Party was formed anyway.

Basically Constitutionalist Libertarians feel the same way, that the 2 party system does more harm than good. All Elections should be non-partisan and people should be allowed to vote in all of the elections both primary and general.

The whiskey tax was repealed in 1802 after Thomas Jefferson's newly named Democratic-Republican Party won the election against Federalist John Adams, who was the only Federalist ever elected. The Federalist Party started to fall apart after Adams was elected in the late 1700s when many of the Federalists joined the Democratic-Republicans, which no doubt was changed to attract them. So the Federalist came to an end in the early 1800s after Jefferson was President.

For a short time the Republicans ended some of the unpopular taxation, but freedom from taxation was short lived because it was later replaced with another luxury tax. This type of tax was called direct tax, because it was a recurring tax paid directly by the taxpayer to the government based on the value of an item. The issue of direct tax as opposed to indirect tax shaped the evolution of the Federal tax policy.

When Thomas Jefferson was elected President in 1802 direct tax was abolished and for the next 10 years there was no internal revenue tax other than excise tax

The reason why the Whiskey Tax did not cause more revolt was a combination of the people being tired of war and some just decided to move outside the boundaries of the US influence and continued to make whiskey. What we do not hear in school is that most of the larger distillers were in favor of the tax, because it put those who couldn't afford it out of business thus stopping much of the competition. Later those larger distillers would band together and work with the government to make only those licensed with the federal government allowed to make whiskey.

Shortly after the demise of the Federalist in the early 1800s came the demise of the Democratic-Republicans. Many of the Federalists had joined the Democratic-Republicans, which was originally just called the Republicans. In 1824 the Democratic-Republican Party dissolved and split into two factions, the Democrats and the Whigs which was inevitable since many of the same disputes arose that did between the Federalist and the Republicans. The Democratic Party was led by the Seventh President of the United States Andrew Jackson and the Eighth President of the United States Martin Van Buren. The Whigs was led by Henry Clay of Kentucky. Both of these parties proclaimed their stand for American Republicanism, but the Democratic Party kept the platform of the Democratic-Republican Party as its own.

The Democratic Party became the majority party, and basically the only party in the United States until shortly before the Civil War. In the 1850's the party split again and those in opposition to slavery left the Democratic Party and helped with the reformation of the Republican Party. The Whig party was pretty much dead and many of the former Whigs finally got assimilated into either the Democrat or Republican Party. In 1910 the Democratic Party regained control of Congress in Washington D.C. and their platform changed once again. They started supporting new progressive ideals and laws, and a more liberal form of government. The Republicans became more conservative and were against the liberal ideals that people like Karl Marx preached in the 1800's. But Marx's philosophy was catching on in America, Europe and especially in Russia where Vladimir Lenin was busy forming what would become the Bolshevik Party a year later in 1911. So the Political Parties basically switched polarity 3 times before becoming what we have today.

Property Tax

In 1796 came the property tax, and all but Delaware imposed a tax on owning property. Delaware only taxed the sale of property, but the road to serfdom was under way. Property Tax was another British Tax that many fought against during the Revolutionary War, and now the new American Government was doing the same to the Citizens. The Citizens didn't mind it quite as much since it was staying in America and not going to the King. They were worried however because the King could take property from subjects whenever he wanted. So many did speak out against this tax but were told the 5th Amendment protected them against the government taking their property without just cause and compensation.

Text of the 5th Amendment Passed on December 15th 1791

"No person shall be held to answer for a capital, or otherwise infamous crime, unless on a presentment or indictment of a Grand Jury, except in cases arising in the land or naval forces, or in the Militia, when in actual service in time of War or public danger; nor shall any person be subject for the same offence to be twice put in jeopardy of life or limb; nor shall be compelled in any criminal case to be a witness against himself, nor be deprived of life, liberty, or property, without due process of law; nor shall private property be taken for public use, without just compensation."

They were also told it was necessary because the State had to document the ownership of the land and record who owned what land so there was no dispute over ownership, and that required paying someone to do that. This gave property value, and gave proof of ownership to who ever had the deed. So then a Value could be placed on that property and compensation would be paid for that property and the government could recognize the property and who the owner(s) were.

This type of record keeping has been done for thousands of years as a way of keeping track of land parcels and the owners. Otherwise anyone could claim they own something and try and sell it to someone else without really owning anything. This also gives the rightful owners help from the government or rulers when someone tries to take property without compensation. So it is helpful to people who worked hard to create a home, farm, ranch or business, put a value on that property and be able to protect it by showing title with a legally recognized Deed.

Unfortunately this once beneficial record keeping practice and acknowledgement of property ownership has been distorted into all out theft by the government of today, and this happened because the citizens allowed it to become an excuse for the better good of society, i.e. "Eminent Domain" and Failing to pay Property Tax.

Taking something from one person and giving it to another you deem more worthy, is exactly what the King of England had done to the colonists, and exactly what dictators and the communist and social fascist do to their citizens.

Thomas Jefferson wrote regarding the "General Welfare" clause: *"To take from one, because it is thought his own industry and that of his father has acquired too much, in order to spare to others who (or whose fathers) have not exercised equal industry and skill, is to violate arbitrarily the first principle of association, to guarantee to everyone a free exercise of his industry and the fruits acquired by it."*

In short if you worked hard to obtain your own property and built a home, farm, ranch and or any business or industry etc, you should not have to share it with anyone; especially lazy people who do not want to work and expect something for nothing!

As America grew there were states and territories that had no property tax and families could live on that land all their lives and then pass it on to their children without the fear of the government taking it from them for failure to pay a tax for something they had worked so hard to create. Today all states have property tax, so anymore you really do not own anything;

you just rent it from the government. If you fail to pay the government for your property, they can take it from you just as the King of England and his Governors had done to the colonists. The Right of Ownership is no Right at all in America today. It is a privilege granted by the Government as long as you can afford to pay them rent for it.

Income Tax

From 1791 to 1802, the United States government was supported by internal taxes on carriages/wagons, distilled spirits, refined sugar, tobacco and snuff, property sold at auction, corporate bonds, and slaves, which were considered a luxury tax on the wealthy. But as the government grew so did its need for more revenue and as the new war with the British approached new taxes were proposed that all Americans would have to pay.

The War of 1812 added sales tax on gold, silverware, jewelry, and watches. The whiskey tax which had come to an end 10 years prior was replaced with other luxury taxes.

In 1817, Congress did away with all internal tariff tax, which relied on tariffs of imported goods from one state to another to provide money for running the government. To raise money for the War of 1812, Congress imposed additional excise tax, raised certain customs duties, and raised money by issuing Treasury notes. For the next 44 years the Federal Government collected no internal revenue. Instead the Government received most of its revenue from high customs duties and excise or luxury tax and through the sale of public land.

But the taxation of gold, silver, and jewelry along with the indirect tax on cotton and other farm products grown in the south was creating a rift in the country that years later would come to a boil. Not all States were going to take the excess of taxation lying down and a rebellion was starting to grow in the States who wanted a return to the Articles of Confederation and out of the United States which they felt had gotten way too controlling. Southerners felt that the Federal government was passing laws and taxes that favored the wealthy industrialists in the north, such as the import tax that treated them unfairly. Many of the Southern plantation owners were Democrats that relied on slave labor for economic success to produce an affordable crop. Their crops were sold to cotton mills in England, and the ships would return with cheap manufactured goods from Europe.

Unfortunately for the Southern States by the early 1800s Northern factories were producing many of the same goods, but at a higher price. So the Northern politicians passed heavy taxes on imported goods from Europe that made the goods so expensive that it was cheaper for the Southerners to buy the more expensive goods from the North. These taxes angered the Southerners because it was obvious to just about everyone what the North and the Federal Government was up to: Revenue Generation Taxation (RGT). They believed that individual states had the right to "nullify", or overturn any law the Federal government passed, which Under the Constitution they should have had. They also believed that individual states had the right to leave the United States and form their own independent country.

But those wealthy industrialists in the North and the Country's newly elected President Abraham Lincoln believed that the concepts of "nullification and state's rights" would make the United States weaker and them poorer, so they were against these ideas and set out to rewrite or to re-interpret the Constitution's 8th and 10th Amendments. In 1860 it all boiled over and the Civil War started and more of our Constitution was shredded when the North defied many of the Rights given the States and the People.

In 1862 in order to support the Civil War effort that the Union was not necessarily winning at the time, the Northern Congress and Abraham Lincoln enacted the nation's first income tax law on those in the Union. It was a forerunner of our income tax today, based on the principles of progressive taxation by withholding income at the source; taking it out of our pay check. This way the government could make sure they got paid. During the Civil War, a person earning from $600 to $10,000 per year paid tax at the rate of only 3%, which wasn't bad compared to today. Those with incomes of more than $10,000 paid tax at a higher rate. Then in 1862 sales and excise tax were added back into law, the very same tax that was abolished by President Jefferson 60 years before in 1802.

Also added to the list of seizure tax was the "inheritance" tax that made its debut in 1862, robbing many families of their homes and property that were unable to pay the tax after a parent or husband had died. On July 1, 1862 the Congress also passed new excise luxury tax on such items as playing cards, gunpowder, feathers, telegrams, iron, leather, pianos, yachts, billiard tables, drugs and patent medicines, and 'whiskey' once again! Even legal documents were taxed. License fees were collected from people for almost all professions, business and trades. In 1866 the internal revenue collections reached their highest point in the nation's 90-year history with more than $310 million dollars being collected and taken from the American Citizens. This was a record until 1911, so it seems that President Abe Lincoln wasn't quite the great American hero portrayed in history, but a Progressive and the greatest taxing President the Country had ever seen at the time; as well as some of the other crimes he committed against the Constitution and Freedom.

The Tax Act of 1862 also established the office of Commissioner of Internal Revenue Services, IRS. The Commissioner was given the power to assess, levy, and collect taxes, and the right to enforce the tax laws through "seizure of property" and income through prosecution. A Right Never Granted to the Federal Government in the Constitution and another deception and lie the American People begrudgingly accepted under the guise it was for the betterment of the Country. This was a way to steal personal property and income without compensation as laid out in the 5th Amendment. The Constitution gives the Congress the power to impose and collect taxes to pay the debts of the government and provide for the common defense and general welfare of the United States, but is subject to the following rules pertaining only to the two classes of taxation permitted, and they are;

1.   DIRECT TAXES, which are subject to the rule of apportionment among the states of the Union.

2.   INDIRECT TAXES, imposts, duties and excises, subject to the rule of uniformity.

Article 1, Section 2, Clause 3 of the Constitution

"Representatives and direct Taxes shall be apportioned among the several States which may be included within this Union, according to their respective Numbers, which shall be determined by adding to the whole Number of free Persons, including those bound to Service for a Term of Years, and excluding Indians not taxed, three fifths of all other Persons. The actual Enumeration shall be made within three Years after the first Meeting of the Congress of the United States, and within every subsequent Term of ten Years, in such Manner as they shall by Law direct. The Number of Representatives shall not exceed one for every thirty Thousand, but each State shall have at Least one Representative; and until such enumeration shall be made, the State of New Hampshire shall be entitled to choose three, Massachusetts eight, Rhode-Island and Providence

Plantations one, Connecticut five, New-York six, New Jersey four, Pennsylvania eight, Delaware one, Maryland six, Virginia ten, North Carolina five, South Carolina five, and Georgia three."

Luckily for those who wanted freedom back in the early years of America there was still a lot of wild country that was not under the government's control. But even in those days many went west to escape the regulations and taxation, because they could not afford to own a place of their own in America. But as the people went west the American government saw some of their possible tax generation escaping and started to incorporate territories that did not belong to them.

The Constitution did not allow the government either one of the two classifications to tax CITIZENS or PERMANENT RESIDENT ALIENS of the United States of America arbitrarily as the new Health-care tax law does. Some groups are exempt while others are forced by threat of fines and imprisonment or death if they refuse to obey.

No where in the Constitution does it give the government the right to force a citizen to buy a product from a private party.

The brief mention of "Direct taxes" in the first sentence of Article 1, Section 2, Clause 3 of the Constitution makes it impossible for the government to use a tax system like the one we have today. It required taxes to be charged by each state's population, rather than by each citizens individual income. In a 5-4 vote, Pollock vs. Farmers Loan Trust Co, the U.S. Supreme Court ruled in 1895 that the income tax is a direct tax. Chief Justice Melville Fuller, writing for the majority, first showed a surprisingly keen awareness of economic concept of incidence: *"Ordinarily, all taxes paid primarily by persons who can shift the burden upon someone else, or who are under no legal compulsion to pay them, are considered indirect taxes; but a tax upon property holders in respect of their estates, whether real or personal, or of the income yielded by such estates, and the payment of which cannot be avoided, are direct taxes."*

He went even further and analyzed the writings of the Framers, the tax writings of Adam Smith, the ratification debates in the states, and observations by early justices and members of Congress. From this he concluded that it was well understood that "all taxes on real estate or personal property or the rents or income there of were regarded as direct taxes."

Since direct taxes must be apportioned by state population under the Constitution, the 1894 law was void. While admitting that such a method of imposing income taxes would be considered unfair by many, its purpose was "to restrain the exercise of the power of direct taxation to extraordinary emergencies, and to prevent an attack upon accumulated property by mere force of numbers." So those in power under the presidencies of republicans Theodore Roosevelt (1901-1909); William H. Taft (1909-1913 and democrat Woodrow Wilson (1913-1921) did what other presidents did to get what they wanted, and that was to cut out the part of our Constitution they didn't like. Since our President appoints the Supreme Court Justice and the House and Senate approve those Supreme Court Justice, they try to appoint people who think like they do to make us believe that they are interpreting the Constitution Legally. But this was nothing more than an illusion and the 16th Amendment was finally past in 1913 to get rid of those pesky Constitutional requirements, making it possible for the government to create the modern income tax system we now have. Individual income tax was never legal under the Constitution, but people were once again threatened and lied to and told by those in power that it was legal, so they begrudgingly paid. There were still Constitutionalists on the

Supreme Court 94 years ago who would later rule against the 16th Amendment, but unfortunately it was ignored just like our supposed representatives do today if they don't like a law or ruling.

Sadly the populace of the United States was never able to directly vote on this, nor did the required three-fourths of the States sign off on this, and it was a proven fact. Because of that one citizen Bill Benson would challenge it almost 90 years later. The federal government rests its authority to collect income tax on the 16th Amendment to the U.S. Constitution, the federal income tax amendment, which was suppose to have been ratified in 1913 after several years of deceptive wrangling to get it to pass.

The 16th Amendment to the Constitution of the United States of America:

"The Congress shall have power to lay and collect taxes on incomes, from whatever source derived, without apportionment among the several States, and without regard to any census or enumeration."

After an extensive year long nationwide research project in 1984, William J. Benson discovered that the 16th Amendment was not ratified by the legally required three fourths of the states and that Secretary of State Philander Knox had fraudulently declared ratification. It was a shocking revelation that reached deep into the core of our American system of government. Even the court system was in on this sham to force citizens to give more to the government. The Government was so annoyed at Bill Benson for exposing this deception that on January 10, 2008, the Federal District Court in Chicago issued a permanent injunction against Bill Benson on the grounds that by offering information demonstrating that the 16th Amendment was not legally ratified by the States, he was promoting an abusive tax shelter. The Court then refused to look at the government-certified documentary evidence, deciding instead that the facts necessary to prove his statements true were "irrelevant." So the American court system has clearly become in league with the politicians and public serpents that make a living from the public dole, and they no longer protect our Rights under the Constitution. Now the government courts routinely accuse citizens of either lying or deeming their arguments as irrelevant and then prohibit them from presenting a defense in court!

If you talk to tax attorneys or other so called tax professionals they will tell you that the 16th Amendment allowed the income tax to be collected as a direct tax without apportionment among the 50 States. This is total BS, and it is the major problem with today's tax collection efforts. Everyone is lied to, and you will comply, because resistance is futile! The IRS believes that the income tax can now be collected as a direct tax without apportionment. It is totally unconstitutional to collect a direct tax in the 50 states without apportionment. So we are the victims of mass brainwashing by the government. But people are waking up and that's why you'll be hearing more politicians talking about a flat tax or a federal sales tax or excise tax, to get around 100 years of Unconstitutional taxation.

So what is Apportion and "Apportionment?"

Black's Law Dictionary says; *Apportion: "To divide and distribute proportionally." Apportionment: "The process by which legislative seats are distributed among units entitled to representation. The U.S. Constitution provides for a census every ten years, on the basis of which Congress apportions representatives according to population; but each state must have at least one representative."*

This gives the people a voice through an elected representative who represents a certain number of citizens in each state.

U. S. CONSTITUTION: *Article 1, Section 2, Clause 3*:

"Representatives and direct taxes shall be apportioned among the states which may be included within this Union, according to their respective numbers..." Article 1, Section 9, Clause 4:"No capitation, or other direct tax, shall be laid, unless in proportion to the census or enumeration herein before directed to be taken."

Direct taxes must be apportioned among the states, not among the people. The 16th Amendment did not change that! The income tax is an excise tax on corporate profit, and always has been therefore it does not need to be apportioned. Before the 16th Amendment, an individual's income was NOT taxable, either with apportionment or without. Eliminating apportionment, among the states, would still require the tax to be imposed on the states, not on the people. This has been a contention for many people over the last century and conflicting rulings have been made by the courts over the years.

In 1920, the Supreme Court said: **Eisner vs Macomber** 252 U.S. 189 at 205 (1920). *"The Sixteenth Amendment must be construed in connection with the taxing clauses of the original Constitution and the effect attributed to them before the Amendment was adopted."*

There it is as Ruled by the Supreme Court! The 16th Amendment had to leave the income tax as an indirect excise tax and should be enforced as such and collected from the states. It is a tax on corporate incomes not requiring the tax to be apportioned on individual citizens! This is not an opinion, but a Supreme Court ruling. An important point to remember is that the Supreme Court rulings must be followed by all lesser courts in this country. They cannot be overruled by lower courts or government officials unless we allow them to get away with it!

The intent of the Founders was to keep the government the servant and to prevent it from becoming the master we have allowed it to become. The People should have a say in their own destiny and were originally meant to through representatives who echoed their concerns. But now most only echo self interest and financial gain and sadly the people allow them to continue their crimes against the Constitution and the people they are supposed to represent.

These Taxes that were the foundation our government used to build its empire are in direct contrast to what our Founding Fathers had in mind. So it does seem that Benjamin Franklin had foreseen what the government he helped to create would one day become, unrecognizable.

As he left the hall in Philadelphia on September 17, 1787, and was asked:

"What kind of government have you given us, Dr. Franklin?" And He replied: *"A republic, if you can keep it."*

In my opinion Franklin, Jefferson, and Madison were the smartest of the group, and saw the danger that Federalists like Hamilton and John Adams would create if not put in check. That is why the Checks and Balances were in the Constitution so no one group could change the rules to affect another group detrimentally. Unfortunately many of those checks and balances have been removed or are totally ignored today and we have a government totally out of control, detrimentally affecting everyone. Many of the founding Fathers were partly responsible for the problem we have today. Founders like John Adams who tried to quietly stack the Courts with 39 new Federalist Justices who would side with him on legal opinion just months before Thomas Jefferson was to take over as President in 1802... That deception infuriated Jefferson, and the divide between the political parties was well underway.

*

Chapter Two

The Laws and Rights That Were Not Granted in the Constitution

There have always been those who want to control, and with that control comes the need for more control. This is pretty much the reason why this country has changed into something it was never intended to become. Most laws were intended to protect not just one individual but to protect all individuals. Unfortunately those who wanted power and control perverted laws to suit their own agendas.

Quaker and Puritan laws were some of the first laws used in early American history. Many of the laws directly came out of the Bible, and if broken, had harsh punishment. Most were meant to humiliate one, like being put in the block, or being chained to a tree where kids would throw crap and tease and torment the law breaker. Harsher punishments were also given like servitude, (enslavement) for a period of time or until the enslaved could pay to be freed. Laws were arbitrary in the colonial period prior to the American Revolution, no distinctive American legal system really existed. Criminal codes, punishments, and courts varied from colony to colony. But in the mid-1700s a national legal set of laws was underway to create a more unified American legal system. The Revolution sped up that process, and the victory over Britain brought independence and a new justice system that provided both protection and rights for American citizens. The first several decades following the Revolution were pretty much an experimental time for criminal justice. Those early court decisions and legislations formed the foundation for the criminal justice system we have now. They had to recognize Rights given each citizen under the State laws and the Constitution first. States wrote up Declarations Of Citizen's Rights, and one of those became the template for the U.S. Constitution.

Virginia's 1776 declaration of rights was the model for the U.S. Bill of Rights, and much of it was added to the U.S. Constitution in 1791, which gave citizens specified Rights. The Virginia Declaration of Rights is a document drafted in 1776 by George Mason to proclaim the inherent rights of men, including the right to rebel against "inadequate" government. Something Abraham Lincoln would later declare treason.

The following is the complete text of the Virginia Declaration of Rights and why George Mason is considered the Father of the Bill of Rights. James Madison is known as the Father of the Constitution, but he and Jefferson consulted George Mason while drafting the US Constitution as their mentor on matters of political theory.

"A DECLARATION OF RIGHTS made by the representatives of the good people of Virginia, assembled in full and free convention which rights do pertain to them and their posterity, as the basis and foundation of government.

Section 1. That all men are by nature equally free and independent and have certain inherent rights, of which, when they enter into a state of society, they cannot, by any compact, deprive or divest their posterity; namely, the enjoyment of life and liberty, with the means of acquiring and possessing property, and pursuing and obtaining happiness and safety.

Section 2. That all power is vested in, and consequently derived from, the people; that magistrates are their trustees and servants and at all times amenable to them.

Section 3. That government is, or ought to be, instituted for the common benefit, protection, and security of the people, nation, or community; of all the various modes and forms of government, that is best which is capable of producing the greatest degree of happiness and safety and is most effectually secured against the danger of maladministration. And that, when any government shall be found inadequate or contrary to these purposes, a majority of the community has an indubitable, inalienable, and indefeasible right to reform, alter, or abolish it, in such manner as shall be judged most conducive to the public weal.

Section 4. That no man, or set of men, is entitled to exclusive or separate emoluments or privileges from the community, but in consideration of public services; which, nor being descendible, neither ought the offices of magistrate, legislator, or judge to be hereditary.

Section 5. That the legislative and executive powers of the state should be separate and distinct from the judiciary; and that the members of the two first may be restrained from oppression, by feeling and participating the burdens of the people, they should, at fixed periods, be reduced to a private station, return into that body from which they were originally taken, and the vacancies be supplied by frequent, certain, and regular elections, in which all, or any part, of the former members, to be again eligible, or ineligible, as the laws shall direct.

Section 6. That elections of members to serve as representatives of the people, in assembly ought to be free; and that all men, having sufficient evidence of permanent common interest with, and attachment to, the community, have the right of suffrage and cannot be taxed or deprived of their property for public uses without their own consent or that of their representatives so elected, nor bound by any law to which they have not, in like manner, assented for the public good.

Section 7. That all power of suspending laws, or the execution of laws, by any authority, without consent of the representatives of the people, is injurious to their rights and ought not to be exercised.

Section 8. That in all capital or criminal prosecutions a man has a right to demand the cause and nature of his accusation, to be confronted with the accusers and witnesses, to call for evidence in his favor, and to a speedy trial by an impartial jury of twelve men of his vicinage, without whose unanimous consent he cannot be found guilty; nor can he be compelled to give evidence against himself; that no man be deprived of his liberty except by the law of the land or the judgment of his peers.

Section 9. That excessive bail ought not to be required, nor excessive fines imposed, nor cruel and unusual punishments inflicted.

Section 10. That general warrants, whereby an officer or messenger may be commanded to search suspected places without evidence of a fact committed, or to seize any person or persons not named, or whose offense is not particularly described and supported by evidence, are grievous and oppressive and ought not to be granted.

Section 11. That in controversies respecting property, and in suits between man and man, the ancient trial by jury is preferable to any other and ought to be held sacred.

Section 12. That the freedom of the press is one of the great bulwarks of liberty, and can never be restrained but by despotic governments.

Section 13. That a well-regulated militia, composed of the body of the people, trained to arms, is the proper, natural, and safe defense of a free state; that standing armies, in time of peace, should be avoided as dangerous to liberty; and that in all cases the military should be under strict subordination to, and governed by, the civil power.

Section 14. That the people have a right to uniform government; and, therefore, that no government separate from or independent of the government of Virginia ought to be erected or established within the limits thereof.

Section 15. That no free government, or the blessings of liberty, can be preserved to any people but by a firm adherence to justice, moderation, temperance, frugality, and virtue and by frequent recurrence to fundamental principles.

Section 16. That religion, or the duty which we owe to our Creator, and the manner of discharging it, can be directed only by reason and conviction, not by force or violence; and therefore all men are equally entitled to the free exercise of religion, according to the dictates of conscience; and that it is the mutual duty of all to practice Christian forbearance, love, and charity toward each other. Written by George Mason, and adopted by the Virginia Constitutional Convention on June 12, 1776."

As you can see by this document, Christian Laws were the foundation of early American laws. But as the country grew so did the laws, many of which were created to address who could own what and where, and laws against vice were created to combat sinful behaviour. But as the country grew, and more laws were created, so did the need to control. Laws were also created that had nothing to do with protecting the people, but to protect the government's control over the people.

Women's Rights

Women's Rights varied from State to State and married women were considered property of their husbands in many of the States. Single women on the other hand had many of the Rights given to males. In every state, the legal status of free women depended upon their marital status. Unmarried women, including widows, were called "femes soles," or "women alone." They had the legal right to live where they pleased and to support themselves in any occupation that did not require a license or a college degree restricted to males. Single women could enter into contracts, buy and sell real estate, or accumulate personal property, which was called *"personalty"*. It consisted of everything from cash, stocks and bonds, livestock, and in the South, slaves. Most of the Northern States abolished slavery after the Revolutionary War. As long as they remained unmarried, they could sue and be sued, write wills, serve as guardians, and act as executors of estates. These rights were a continuation of the colonial legal tradition. But the revolutionary emphasis on equality brought some important changes in women's inheritance rights. State lawmakers everywhere abolished primogeniture and the tradition of double shares of a parent's estate, inheritance customs that favored the eldest son. Instead, equal inheritance for all children became the rule which was a big gain for daughters.

Women were not allowed to vote or hold office until 1920 when the 19th Amendment was passed. Women were also not allowed by law to tend a bar right up to the mid 1970s. One such law was passed in Michigan in 1945 making it illegal for a woman, with the exception of the wife or daughter of the saloon keeper, to mix drinks behind the bar. Valentine Goesaert and three other women from Michigan challenged the statute as unconstitutional, taking their case all the way to the Supreme Court. Writing the majority opinion in Goesaert v. Cleary in 1948 was, Associate Justice of the Supreme Court Felix Frankfurter (1939-1962) who seemed downright amused that anyone would think the "equal-protection" clause of the 14th Amendment would apply to women and cocktails. Despite the centuries of old tradition of "sprightly and ribald" alewives, Frankfurter wrote, ***"Michigan could, beyond question, forbid*** *all women from working behind a bar."* Frankfurter was a progressive that was also a stickler for respecting the prerogative of state legislature and courts, and he even gave a wink and a nudge to indicate that he knew exactly what the law was all about.

The court, he wrote; *"cannot give ear to the suggestion that the real impulse behind this legislation was an unchivalrous desire of male bartenders to try to monopolize the calling."*

Michigan dropped the law in 1955, but other states had similar restrictions on the books. In 1971 California still officially barred women from "pouring whiskey." The court case that finally overturned that state law involved a topless bar called Sail'er Inn, which wanted to move some dancers behind the bar to mix drinks.

Craig v. Boren, 429 U.S. 190 (1976), was the first case in which a majority of the United States Supreme Court determined that statutory or administrative sex classifications had to be subjected to an intermediate standard of judicial review.

Voting Laws

The Right to vote was not allowed for all citizens until restrictions were lifted about 40 years ago. In many places people had to prove they were intelligent enough in politics to be able to vote. It was later deemed discriminatory and was abolished. When you come to think of it maybe that might have been a big mistake because people should really know what is going on in politics before they vote; all too often people just go in blindly without a clue as to what or who they are voting on or for. I liken it to allowing a person to drive a car or fly a plane without ever learning how. This may sound a bit harsh; but when we allow a dictator to get elected just because he or she is a certain color or gender that we may like. Or they just might be mister or miss popular at the time, and we really do not even know who they are, or what they really believe in or stand for, we could be in for some big trouble which has been the fall of many a nation. If we the voters do not start to read, learn and understand our Constitution; and we do not also start to realize that this document was put in place for us to keep our freedom, and we keep electing people whose main goal is to shred it… Then our country is doomed for disaster and is destined to fail as history has seen before!

Here are some of the Voting Laws from 1776 to Today

1776-1787: Declaration of Independence ("All men are created equal"), Articles of Confederation, U.S. Constitution leave voting rights to state jurisdiction. "Suffrage" = (Right to vote) is limited to white male property owners.

1776-1807: New Jersey women, age 21 and over, can vote if they fulfill residency and property requirements. In 1807 the New Jersey legislature rescinds women's suffrage.

1776: Free black men can vote in New Jersey, Pennsylvania and Connecticut.

1792-1838: The Constitutions of Connecticut, Delaware, Kentucky, Maryland, New Jersey, North Carolina, Tennessee, and Virginia, were changed ending the black male voting Right and exclude blacks from voting but expand white male suffrage.

1848: The Treaty of Guadalupe-Hidalgo ends the Mexican-American War and guarantees U.S. citizenship to Mexicans living in the newly acquired territories of Arizona, California, Colorado, New Mexico, Nevada and Texas. English language requirements limit their access to voting rights.

1860: Five states (Maine, New Hampshire, Vermont, Rhode Island, and Massachusetts) allow free black men to vote.

1867: Kansas holds the first referendum on women's suffrage in the U.S. The measure fails.

1869: Wyoming Territorial legislature grants full voting rights to women. Wyoming was not yet a State

1870: Utah Territorial legislature grants full voting rights to women. Utah was not yet a State.

1870: Passage of the 15th Amendment prohibits states from denying citizens the vote based on "race, color, or previous condition of servitude," but many Blacks, Asians, and Hispanics remain disfranchised in the South by poll taxes and literacy tests.

1882: The Chinese Exclusion Act bars people of Chinese ancestry from becoming American citizens.

1883: Washington Territorial legislature grants full voting rights to women. Washington was not yet a State.

1884: The U.S. Supreme Court rules, in Elk vs. Wilkins, that Native Americans are not citizens as defined by the 14th Amendment.

1887: Passage of the Dawes Act grants citizenship to Native Americans who give up their tribal affiliations. U.S. Congress rescinds women's suffrage in Utah. The Territorial Supreme Court rescinds women's suffrage in Washington Territory.

1888: Act of 1888 grants citizenship to Indian women who marry white men. Washington Territorial legislature grants women the right to vote but the Territory's Supreme Court quickly rescinds that right, for the second time.

1889: Washington state referendum defeats women's suffrage.

1890: Wyoming enters the Union as the first state granting full women's suffrage (Right to Vote) in State Elections. Also in 1890 on a National level; The Indian Naturalization Act grants citizenship to American Indians whose applications are approved (similar to the process of immigrant naturalization). But many Indians and part Indians do not apply because they were treated worse than Blacks and had Bounties from 5 to 10 dollars put on their children who were forced to go to Government approved schools.

1893: Colorado state referendum grants full voting rights to women.

1896: Utah and Idaho grant full voting rights to women.

1901: Congress grants citizenship to Indians living in Indian Territory (Oklahoma).

1910: Washington state referendum approves full suffrage for women.

1911: California state referendum approves full voting rights for women.

1912: Oregon, Kansas and Arizona state referenda approve full voting rights for women.

1913: Alaska Territorial Legislature approves women's right to vote as its first official act.

1914: Montana and Nevada referenda approve full suffrage for women.

1918: South Dakota and Oklahoma referenda grant full suffrage to women.

1919: American Indians who served in the military during World War I are granted U.S. citizenship.

1920: U.S. House of Representatives and Senate approve the 19th Amendment to grant suffrage (Right to Vote) to women. Amendment wins the necessary 2/3 ratification from state legislatures.

1922: Supreme Court rules, in Takao Ozawa v. United States, that people of Japanese heritage are not eligible to become naturalized citizens.

1924: The Indian Citizenship Act grants citizenship to American Indians, but many western states prohibited their voting.

1925: Filipinos barred from citizenship unless they have served three years in the U.S. Navy.

1943: Chinese Exclusion Act is repealed, making people of Chinese ancestry eligible for U.S. citizenship.

1946: Filipinos and indigenous people from India become eligible for U.S. citizenship.

1952: Walter-McCarran Act grants all people of Asian ancestry the right to become citizens.

1953: Full suffrage approved in New Mexico.

1965: The Voting Rights Act of 1965 suspends literacy tests in the Deep South and provides federal enforcement of black registration and voting rights where denied.

1970: The 1970 Voting Rights Act bans literacy tests in 20 states, including New York, Illinois, and California.

1971: The passage of the 26th Amendment expands full voting rights to 18 year-old citizens.

1975: 1975 Voting Rights Act provides language assistance to minority voters.

As you can see, not everyone had the Right to vote in America and only just within the last 45 years have the laws and limitations been lifted to allow all legal citizens in good standing, (Without Felonies or Crimes against the Country), a Right to vote. The irony in this is, less people choose to use the Right to Vote now that they have won the Right to do so, and 80% of those who vote believe just about anything they hear.

Another interesting fact is that when times are bad and people are out of work, the people with a little political knowledge will convince those who know nothing to vote for the Socialists so they can get free money i.e. "Entitlements" and when times are good and there are plenty of jobs and everyone is making plenty of money, people will convince those who know nothing to vote for Conservatives because they don't want to give the Government any of their money to pay for those entitlements. This impulse voting without knowing what damage will be done is why we are losing freedom.

"The policy of the American Government is to leave its citizens free, neither restraining them nor aiding them in their pursuits" – Thomas Jefferson

**

Chapter Three

Laws, Rules and Actions that Cost Us "Freedom"

There are so many laws and rules on the books in this country that I could go on and on, so I will try and limit them to some of the most important ones that have cost us a lot of our freedom. Many of our freedoms were lost in just the last 35 years. Some of you younger readers may never have known we had these freedoms. That is because those who were against those freedoms never want you to know they were taken, or changed, to make you believe they are now a privilege and not a Right.

According to the Constitution the Rights that were given to us can not legally be taken away. But we allowed our government to pull the wool over our eyes while they added restrictions and changed the meaning of many of those Rights. This has been a major cause of our freedom lost. Unfortunately many of our Rights have turned into a Privilege or have just been totally ignored.

Most Americans think we have protection from an abusive government because of the Constitution and The Bill of Rights.

Sadly we really have no protection at all. Our judges and police have no use for the Constitution or the Bill of Rights and routinely tell anyone who quotes any part of the document that they are out of order and to keep their mouth shut or they will be held in contempt of court and/or arrested for P.O.P. pissing off police! The majority of people cower in fear and allow themselves to be abused, even when they know they are innocent and have Rights granted them in the Constitution. Unfortunately though, the people who stand their ground and bring up our Rights under the Constitution, really make the gestapo/police mad. The police know we are right and they can't stand it! They will try and twist our words around and then use them against us to abuse and arrest us. After you are arrested and put in jail, you will usually be threatened with a long jail sentence if you don't cop a plea to a crime that you never even commit. As outrageous as this sounds it does not stop there. If you dare go to the press to let the public know the abuse of power that has been committed against you and take your case to court. The Court will paint you as the bad guy who does not know what they are talking about and persuade a jury to convict you. The Judge will come down hard on anyone who dares to try and show the people that the government thinks they are above the law and does not respect our Constitutional

Rights!   But the Constitution and Bill of Rights gives us the Right to Question their Authority.

I've learned a lot of what I wrote above from the many people who have come to me and shared their story of abuse of power by their city officials, when I was on the city council and the publisher of The Nor-Cal Paper. I published their story in my newspaper without judgement. I was an open forum newspaper where anyone could have a say. I attended many of the court hearings of the stories I published, and I witnessed first hand the abusive way the court would treat the people; and sometimes even me just for attending.

These are your Rights that you should never allow to be taken or changed into a privilege!

The First Amendment:

"Congress shall make no law respecting an establishment of religion, or prohibiting the free exercise thereof; or abridging the freedom of speech, or of the press; or the right of the people peaceably to assemble, and to petition the Government for a redress of grievances."

The Right of free speech and religion is a classic example of Rights that have been lost by added rules and laws governing those Rights. We no longer have the 1st Amendment as it was intended. Now you must follow certain rules and laws governing religion and speech or you can be arrested, fined and or imprisoned.

A classic example was the arrest of two men who started to read the bible out loud in the parking lot of a DMV office in California several years ago. There was also the arrest and conviction a couple years ago of two brothers, Benjamin and Russell Bartholomew of Wheatland, Calif. who were protesting taxes in Yuba County, Calif. The Yuba County Sheriff and CHP saw a chance to get around their Constitutional right to protest by charging the two for wearing masks. The brothers had on masks as a form of political theater. It was the same mask that had become a symbol of revolt popularized in the movie V for Vendetta. The law states anyone who wears a mask while committing a crime is a violation; but these two were not committing a crime, they were Protesting Taxes. This was just another tactic the Gestapo could use to detain them. The District Attorney knew this would not stand up in court, so after a lot of research, the charge was changed to detaining an Officer from performing their duties, PC148, which was also totally bogus. The two brothers had videoed the whole incident with the sheriffs and CHP live via direct upload to their You Tube site;

goodmendosomething.org and on You Tube at: http://www.youtube.com/watch?v=sG0rAkTJDmQ&feature=c4 -overview-vl&list=PLE2114D1A87F51B0F

Picture taken at second protest in Yuba County, California.

No one ever thought a jury would convict these two, but after the district attorney did his research and found a legal precedence that allowed them to arrest any protesters who

Detained an Officer in the performance of their duties they charged and convicted the two young men because the Sheriff and CHP had to confront and harrass the two protesters. This was a classic case of being charged with "P.O.P. - Pissing Off Police". The irony in all of this was a Yuba County Jury convicted the two brothers of basically Protesting Taxes, along with the crime Yuba County fabricated, which gave them a reason to arrest and charge the two, which was PC148. In the court trial one of the officers involved even stated under oath that he was wrong in arresting them for the charge, and yet the brainwashed jury still convicted these two brothers for what basically was protesting taxes. The Jury was not allowed to view the entire video and were basically told they had to convict the two young men, and that is exactly what they did. At their sentencing their father who was a Major in the USAF at that time, read a speech questioning what he was fighting for in America and stated his sons were doing more for freedom than he had in his whole time with the military. It was a speech reminiscent to Patrick Henry's Give me liberty or give me death and after he was done reading it, I applauded and was promptly thrown out of the Courtroom for my outburst of public courtroom disobedience. No longer can anyone in a courtroom move, speak out, talk, motion, nod, applaud or even wipe a runny nose without getting thrown out.

Justice in America has become a joke complete with little tin-gods that rule us as if they are God. No more order in the court spouted by the judge, just the 4 or 5 bailiffs with guns running over and forcefully removing the people who speak out or motion in any way. They surely don't want people to disagree with the judge and agree with the accused. Sadly most jurors have no idea what jury nullification is; *(A Jury Voting Not Guilty if they don't agree with a crime against the defendant).* Most jurors have no idea what abuse some Judges commit against a defendant and they really don't care. There are People that don't even know that a judge can be recalled by the citizens if they feel he or she isn't following the oath that the judge swore when they were elected. When they are sworn in, they promise to uphold the Constitution of the USA and the State they are in. The words "Blind Justice" now take on a whole new meaning in America.

Shortly after the two Brothers were sentenced and fined they went back to the same place and performed the same Protest with an even larger Taxes=Theft sign. Only this time there were many more people with them and several Medias from newspapers to TV stations… and you know what? The local Law Enforcers did nothing this time!

This goes to show there is power in numbers and our laws in America are arbitrarily enforced or fabricated to suit the government. Unfortunately the brothers didn't appeal their conviction to a higher court because of unknown reasons. They were even told there were attorneys standing by pro-bono if they wanted to fight it. Well whatever the reason they still made an impact, but because they didn't appeal the conviction and win on appeal, this is now a California precedent that can be quoted in other Protest cases.

About the same time this was going on back in 2011 and 2012, a former Marysville City Councilman was running for Yuba County Judge. This person had repeatedly called me a Nazi because I was at the time the Chair of the Yuba County Libertarian Party, and was against him ever becoming a Judge. No One Should Ever Be Allowed To Sit On A Legal Bench who calls someone a Nazi for believing in Liberty and Justice For All! He even threatened the owner of the local AM Radio Station that was supporting my efforts and told him that he would never run any political ads with the station as long as he supported Nazi Libertarians like myself. The local daily newspaper knew about this and said nothing. Many other medias in the Yuba-Sutter area also knew and said nothing! This supposed honest and just person used the Nazi propaganda to discredit my opinion of his performance while on the City Council, and because the local media wanted his ad money, they reported the news by omission and he won the election and is now a Yuba County Superior Court Judge! I know… it is really scary and hard to believe, but people did elect Obama… twice! Unfortunately most of the medias omitted the negative information that most certainly would have lost him the election!

Both Religion and Tax Protest cases clearly are a Right under the First Amendment, but the government sidestepped the Constitution by sighting other California Laws to charge the people with. Clearly doing an end run around the people's Rights alleging the California Laws supersede the Constitution and therefore canceling out the people's Constitutional Rights. Yet government attorneys and judges will argue these cases have nothing to do with Constitutional Rights and claim they are legally justified to charge people and convict them. Sadly the majority of the sheeple believe them, and the people that don't believe will rarely speak out.

If an individual that reads the Bible out loud and/or Protest taxes are not utilizing their Constitutional Right according to California Law Enforcers; then this would be a classic example of taking our First Amendment Right and turning it into a Privilege complete with rules and secondary laws to back up those rules, making the First Amendment void in California or at best arbitrarily allowed. This isn't a California issue alone by any means, it happens all across the country. But California by far is one of the worst states that are destroying our Constitutional Rights in the Nation. They are followed by New York. They are two of the most populated states which set the stage for the federal government to change the meaning or our Rights.

Many of our States deliberately refuse to allow people to enjoy their Constitutional Rights, especially when the government in control disapproves of a Right Granted in the Bill of Rights, such as the Second Amendment.

Second Amendment in the Bill of Rights:

You can judge for yourselves what our Founding Fathers had in mind when they wrote the Second Amendment.

As passed by Congress and preserved in the National Archives: *"A well regulated Militia, being necessary to the security of a free State, the right of the people to keep and bear Arms, shall not be infringed."*

This once guaranteed Right has now also been labeled a Privilege complete with laws and rules that totally go against the Second Amendment. Thirty years ago you could buy a hand gun or rifle from most anyone, anywhere in California. You could even walk down the end of a street in most parts of California into the fields, forest, deserts and wild lands with your gun to go hunting or target practice without anyone going through convulsions over it. Then the Progressives and Socialists got control and spat on the Constitution and started the Infringement of the Second Amendment.

The Second Amendment clearly states that the "RIGHT" to bear arms "SHALL NOT BE INFRINGED" yet in California they recently passed a no open carry law against all Guns. This means if you openly carry a gun in public and show it, use it, sell it, or do not register or buy it through a STATE LICENSED DEALER; It can and will be used against you in a court of law that will make you out to look like a criminal, and then they will take away your RIGHT TO BEAR ARMS; But when you come to think about it we really have already lost that right! The politicians and law enforcers who work fervently to try and convince the people that this is not INFRINGING on their Rights honestly believe that The People are that stupid and will fall for it. Unfortunately they have been proven right, because the people really have done nothing to stop this Unconstitutional downright outward theft and abuse of our second amendment Right.

Elected officials like Dianne Feinstein a US Senator from California, and State Senator Darrel Steinberg, really seem to hate the Constitution. They especially hate the Second Amendment. Feinstein and Steinberg have repeatedly tried to destroy the Second Amendment and Feinstein stated in a media interview; *"If I could have gotten 51 votes in the Senate I would have said Mr. and Mrs. America turn in your guns."* - Dianne Feinstein told the interviewer this after her failed attempts to repeal the Second Amendment. They now are going after ammunition, and have passed a law banning lead bullets in California. How the hell is that not infringing on our Right to Bear Arms?

People in the government like Feinstein, Steinberg, Boxer, Pelosi and Obama, and in the socialist media like British commentator Piers Morgan work tirelessly to destroy the Constitution by using fear and bogus statistics to sway public opinion and to disarm Americans and further enslave them.

Let's look at some facts and recorded cause of deaths annually in the country according to our government's own statistics.

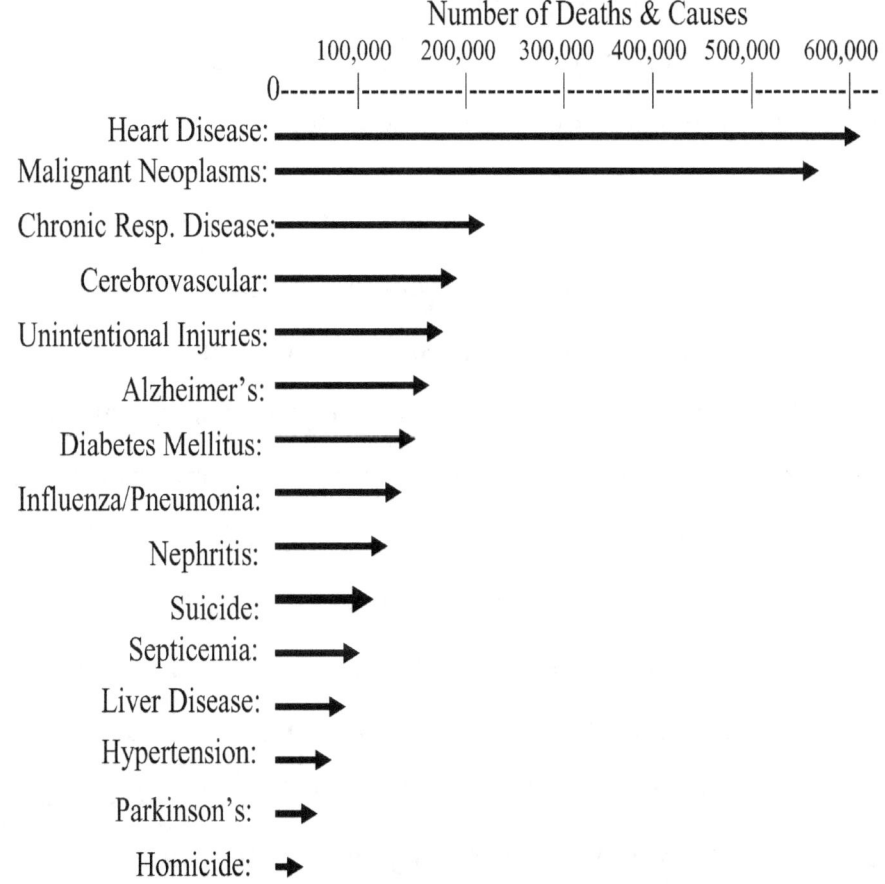

Number of Deaths & Causes

Number One Killer is Heart Disease 597,689 – Number Two: Cancer 574,743 – Number Three: Chronic lower Respiratory

Disease 138,080 – Number Four: Stroke 129,476 – Number Five: Accidents 120,859 – Number Six: Alzheimer's 83,494 – Number Seven: Diabetes 69,071 – Number Eight: Nephritis 50,476 – Number Nine: Influenza & Pneumonia 50,097 – Number Ten: Suicide 38,364. The statistics above are from 2010. They were the most complete and available statistics that I could find. The total number of deaths by "guns" recorded back in 2010 was only 9,146 which also included people killed by law enforcers, suicide and self defense.

Knives, hands, feet and clubs account for more murders than rifles in America. Rifles only account for 384 deaths compared to 1,825 people who were killed by knives and sharp cutting tools. 801 people were killed by other people using their hands, fists and feet, 611 people were killed by blunt objects like bats, clubs, and hammers. There is a substantial difference when you compare all of this to the 384 people killed by rifles. I use the rifle statistics because the media and socialists in our government seem to be chipping away at our Second Amendment by using Rifles or (Assault Rifles) as they like to call them. They have successfully gained control of the hand guns with their laws that circumvent the Second Amendment which has made it too expensive and/or too regulated for most citizens to afford or be approved to legally bear those arms.

This picture from the internet asks a very good question. Why do we need these armored tanks to direct traffic and why is the government trying to disarm us?

The US Government has totally ignored the Constitution when it comes to our Second Amendment Right. They have allowed States like California and New York to violate the Constitution with contempt. Many will argue that the Second Amendment is mostly still intact, but it is not! The 1968 Federal Gun Control Act shown below proves how the Second Amendment has been whittled down over the years:

"Under the United States Gun Control Act of 1968, any cartridge firearm made in or before 1898 ("pre-1899") is classified as an "antique", and is generally outside of Federal jurisdiction, as administered and enforced by the U.S. Bureau of Alcohol, Tobacco, Firearms and Explosives (BATFE). The only exceptions to the Federal exemption are antique machineguns (such as the Maxim gun and Colt Model 1895 "Potato Digger") and antique cartridge rifles or shotguns firing shotgun shells that are classified as "short barreled" per the U.S. Gun Control Act of 1968, namely cartridge rifles with a barrel less than 16 inches long, or shotguns firing shotgun shells with a barrel less than 18 inches long, or either cartridge rifles or shotgun-shell-firing shotguns with an overall length of less than 26 inches. Muzzleloading guns, as replicas of antique guns, are not subject to Federal jurisdiction and are essentially classified the same as an antique gun. Hence, a muzzleloading black-powder shotgun is not subject to the short-barreled National Firearms Act of 1934 restrictions. Purchases of such modern-day manufactured replicas may be done outside of the normal Federal Firearms License (FFL) restrictions that otherwise exist when purchasing modern (post-1898) guns. Replicas of cartridge-firing rifles, however, are not classed the same as

antiques, but must be purchased through FFL holders, although a true antique that was manufactured prior to 1899 firing the same cartridge as the replica would be legal for sale without the transfer being processed through an FFL. Furthermore, any rifle re-built on a receiver or frame that was manufactured prior to 1899 is considered antique, even if it has been re-barreled or even if every other part has been replaced.

The following is an excerpt from the portion of the Gun Control Act of 1968 (which modified Title 18, U.S. Code) that exempted pre-1899 guns from the Federal Firearms License paperwork requirements administered by the BATFE:

18 USC 921 (a)(16). (A) any firearm (including any firearm with a matchlock, flintlock, percussion cap, or similar type of ignition system) manufactured in or before 1898; and (B) any replica of any firearm described in subparagraph (A) if such replica -- (i) is not designed or redesigned for using rimfire or conventional centerfire fixed ammunition, or (ii) uses rimfire or conventional centerfire fixed ammunition which is no longer manufactured in the United States and which is not readily available in the ordinary channels of commercial trade.

Within the United States, antique exemptions vary considerably from state to state.

Identifying pre-1899 antiques

The production of many cartridge firearms, such as the famous Winchester Model 1894 lever action rifle took place both before and after the December 31, 1898 cut-off date that delineates exempt antique status under U.S. law. Therefore, collectors rely on references such as The Pre-1899 Antique Guns FAQ by James Wesley Rawles to determine if a particular gun's serial number falls within the range of "antique" (pre-1899) production. For example, a Winchester Model 1894 with serial number 147,685 had its frame (or "receiver") made in December 1898 and it is hence classified as an "antique", but records show that a Winchester Model 1894 with serial number 147,686 had its frame made in January, 1899 and it is hence classified as "modern" by the BATFE therefore, black powder weapons are not firearms unless said black powder weapon can be converted to propel rim-fire ammunition.

Since it is the date of manufacture of the receiver that is relevant to identifying a gun as antique or modern, it is possible to have a weapon with date marks post-1898 but still be considered an antique gun. For example, some Finnish M39 (Ukko-Pekka) Mosin-Nagant rifles with hexagonal profile receivers are considered antique because some were built on receivers dated pre-1899, even though the rifle itself was adopted in 1939. Many of these were assembled using a mix of old round and "hex" receivers from then on, until as late as the 1970s. To be identified as pre-1899, however, Mosin-Nagants that have been re-barreled must be disassembled to see the date stamps on their tangs. A similar situation exists for 7.65mm Mauser Turkish Model 1893 bolt actions, most of which were re-arsenalized at the Ankara arsenal in the 1940s, and re-chambered to 8x57mm Mauser. Despite this re-arsenalization and re-chambering, they are still considered antiques under US law as all rifles of that model were manufactured between 1893 and 1896. Likewise, all firearms produced by Ludwig Loewe & Co. A.G., which are marked "Ludwig Loewe" or "Loewe, Berlin", are antiques. This is because Ludwig Loewe was merged into Deutsche Waffen und Munitionsfabriken in 1897, and the Loewe name was no longer used after the merger.

In the case United States vs. Kirvan, He was charged with Armed Robbery and a Felon in possession of a firearm while committing a felony. Kirvan was found guilty of the armed robbery but was found innocent of being a felon in possession of a firearm while committing a felony charge; due to the fact that a black powder weapon is not considered a firearm under the definition of federal gun laws. It was added that a black powder weapon that has never been used or shot before, classifies it as a display piece which does not consider it a firearm. Therefore the judge had to dismiss the charge.

So now only Black Powder guns are legal under the Second Amendment in the Constitution according to the Federal Government. They have been totally against what the Second Amendment stands for and have been trying to change the meaning of the Amendment for well over 150 years. After all their toiling with no surprise, they have successfully managed to change our second amendment and believe me they are not done yet!

In United States v. Cruikshank, 92 U.S. 542 (1875), the Supreme Court ruled that; *"The right to bear arms is not granted by the Constitution; neither is it in any manner dependent upon that instrument for its existence. The Second Amendment means no more than that it shall not be infringed by Congress, and has no other effect than to restrict the powers of the 'National Government.'"* This was shortly after the Civil War and the government was eager to limit the people's ability to wage war against the government ever again.

Other Supreme Court Cases that further confused the Second Amendment Right are: In the *District of Columbia v. Heller*, 554 U.S. 570 (2008**)**, the Supreme Court ruled that the Second Amendment ***"Codified a pre-existing Right"*** and that it protects an individuals Right to possess a firearm unconnected with service in a militia, and to use that arm for traditional lawful purpose, such as self-defense within the home. It also stated; *"that the right is not unlimited. It is not a right to keep and carry any weapon whatsoever in any manner whatsoever and for whatever purpose".* They also clarified that many longstanding prohibitions and restrictions on firearm possession listed by the Court are consistent with the Second Amendment. Which is just manipulation of the Constitution to control the Right!

In *McDonald v. Chicago*, 561 U.S. 3025 (2010), the Supreme Court ruled that the Second Amendment limits state and local government to the same extent that it limits the federal government.

This hasn't stopped the State and Federal government from issuing laws and rules attached to our Constitutional Right under the Second Amendment. The government both federal and state, have for the most part ignored High Court rulings because they know it takes a lot of resource and a long time for anyone or any group to get a challenge to the Supreme Court, and by the time they do, most people will have excepted whatever illegal unconstitutional law that has been imposed and enforced on them. Only the Government (Federal & State) or large corporatations with the financial resource are able to fight in the High Court arena, unless public outcry is widespread, and then the High Court may rule on the issue.

Our Government seems to be able to change so many of our rights at the drop of a dime. If it can help them win a case or they just want to exude their power and show us they are our masters, they will do whatever is necessary to win! We The Citizens of America need to be able to Amend our Constitution to allow The Supreme Court Justice to be overruled if three fourths of the State disagree with their ruling. Then it should go to a vote of the people to either invalidate or ratify. This would give back the state their right that was granted them under the 10th Amendment of the Constitution; especially since we have seen totally Unconstitutional Laws/Taxes passed by the Supreme Court over the years. The Supreme Court Justice should have a term limit just as the President does, the reasoning behind this is pretty obvious. When an official is elected and they turn out to be bad and pass unconstitutional laws and regulations. We need to be able to get them out or have some solace in knowing that their time is limited. The President is only elected for a 4 year term and can do a lot of damage in that time, but we can choose to not elect them again in the next term. A Justice is in there for life and can really make some bad judgements that could shatter our constitutional rights, and when they do there is no way to get them out, or change their ruling!

This was the ratified wording from the States and authenticated by Thomas Jefferson, then Secretary of State: *"A well regulated militia being necessary to the security of a free state, the right of the people to keep and bear arms shall not be infringed."*

Free people should not have to ask for permission in a free country, especially when it comes down to your Guaranteed Amendment Rights! This is something you might think about if you ever have to ask permission from your government to use a Guaranteed Freedom that was clearly defined in the Bill of Rights as part of the Constitution. If any of your government officials laugh at you when you even mention your rights, ask them if they swore an oath to uphold the Constitution. If they did, then why are they laughing?

The Third Amendment:

"No Soldier shall, in time of peace be quartered in any house, without the consent of the Owner, nor in time of war, but in a manner to be prescribed by law."

The Third Amendment to the United States Constitution places restrictions on the quartering of soldiers in private homes without the owner's consent, forbidding the practice in peace time. The amendment is a response to Quartering Acts passed by the British parliament during the American Revolutionary War that allowed the British Army to lodge soldiers in private residences. Basically they would take a persons home and use it for as long as it was in their interest and loot it and many times burn it to the ground.

But today the government can easily get around the Third Amendment by declaring marshal law against an unknown terrorist which they claim they are at war with.

Fourth Amendment:

"The right of the people to be secure in their persons, houses, papers, and effects, against unreasonable searches and seizures, shall not be violated, and no Warrants shall issue, but upon probable cause, supported by Oath or affirmation, and particularly describing the place to be searched, and the persons or things to be seized."

The Fourth Amendment governing search and seizure has been shredded and is basically just words with no meaning as far as the government is concerned. It is supposed to prohibit unreasonable search and seizure and requires a warrant to be judicially sanctioned by a Judge and supported by probable cause. It was adopted in response to the abuse of the writ of assistance, a type of general search warrant issued by the British Government and a major source of tension in pre-Revolutionary America. The government of today has reintroduced the Writ of Assistance by allowing a Judge to sign a blank warrant that law enforcers can use without contacting a judge. These warrants are a Blanket Warrant that covers everything and anything, just like the Gestapo used in Nazi Germany.

This very important Right is ignored by most of the States and the Federal Government, and of all the Amendments I think this one has been abused the most by our government. Sadly it is each and every one of our faults, because we have done nothing to stop the abuse. We allow these liars and power hungry manipulators to stay in power, even after they have proven they have no intention of representing the people that they were elected to represent or protect the Constitution… Whenever an honest person does manage to get elected and they try to do the right things that an elected official is suppose to do, they are bad mouthed in the socialist media and by every anti-constitutional and communist group infesting this Country! Even other politicians will bad mouth the honest politician if they rock the boat and upset their gravy train. Consequently it is the honest politicians who don't last long in politics, and that is the biggest shame, because the uninformed and ignorant people believe the lies and they side with the tyrants.

The Fifth Amendment:

"No person shall be held to answer for a capital, or otherwise infamous crime, unless on a presentment or indictment of a Grand Jury, except in cases arising in the land or naval forces, or in the Militia, when in actual service

in time of War or public danger; nor shall any person be subject for the same offence to be twice put in jeopardy of life or limb; nor shall be compelled in any criminal case to be a witness against himself, nor be deprived of life, liberty, or property, without due process of law; nor shall private property be taken for public use, without just compensation."

The Fifth Amendment has been ignored and has been deemed as Not a Defense in court after court. This Amendment is extremely important to Freedom and people have stood aside and said nothing, allowing it to become null and void. I have seen people attempt to use their 4th and 5th Amendment Rights when being abused by Law Enforcers. These law enforcers who swore an oath to uphold the Constitution and Bill of Rights, just laugh between each other and say, Ha, he thinks he knows his Rights, we'll show him how much he knows." Then they arrest that person without just cause. The Gestapo calls this a P.O.P. charge as I stated earlier, which if you forgot means (Pissing Off Police).

Judges have totally thrown out the 5th Amendment defense in most cases and force people to talk by intimidation of contempt, jail time and fines. I have heard judges tell defendants who try and use the 5th Amendment that it doesn't apply in their case and they had to talk or they would be jailed for contempt of court. On the other hand I have also heard defense attorneys say that they have to see the same Judges in their courtroom day after day, so they have to watch what they say, even if the Judge is totally wrong and the defendant has the 5th Amendment Right on their side. The attorney does not want to piss off the judge by objecting. I have come to the realization that if you want an attorney who will not be scared of pissing off the judge, you have to go outside your local area to find one.

The Sixth Amendment:

"In all criminal prosecutions, the accused shall enjoy the right to a speedy and public trial, by an impartial jury of the State and district wherein the crime shall have been committed, which district shall have been previously ascertained by law, and to be informed of the nature and cause of the accusation; to be confronted with the witnesses against him; to have compulsory process for obtaining witnesses in his favor, and to have the Assistance of Counsel for his defence."

I don't think you have to look too far to see this Amendment has also been shredded and twisted to serve the courts and not those accused of a crime. Since the advent of the cell phone and video cameras, more and more people are video taping crimes by both citizen and law enforcers, and time and time again police seize the recording device and erase or destroy them which is directly in violation of the 1st, 4th and 5th Amendments. The Courts are also refusing to allow many of these recorded violations to be seen, especially if it shows law enforcers are the ones breaking the law with civil Rights violations.

The Seventh Amendment:

"In Suits at common law, where the value in controversy shall exceed twenty dollars, the right of trial by jury shall be preserved, and no fact tried by a jury, shall be otherwise re-examined in any Court of the United States, than according to the rules of the common law."

Once again the 7th Amendment is also ignored and maybe the most ignored by far. Anytime you see "mandatory arbitration" in any warrantee on any item you buy, or when signing up for telephone service, cable, gas and electric, or even signing to be seen by a doctor, or buying a new car, you are signing away your 7th Amendment Right, and the odds are stacked against you. Most times you have no recourse to appeal a decision and it's stated that all decisions are final.

The right to file a civil complaint in federal court has been shredded by the Supreme Court's decision on *Iqbal* and the *Twombly* cases. I have to wonder if this wasn't deliberate since it created new harder standards for filing a civil suit against a corporation, and it will no doubt get worse with the new interpretations/rewriting of the 7th Amendment each time one of the appeal courts get to it. The 7th shredding started in 1950 with a Supreme Court decision that pretty much gives governments and government contractors exemption from being sued for negligence. Trying to recover from negligence at the hands of the government or military or a government contractor with billions of dollars in government contracts probably isn't going to happen no matter how blatant the negligence was. So the Corporate Government has made sure it's protected from the people by changing the rules contrary to what the 7th Amendment of the Constitution clearly states… And once again the people are complacently apathetic about all this manipulation of the Bill of Rights.

The Eighth Amendment:

"Excessive bail shall not be required, nor excessive fines imposed, nor cruel and unusual punishments inflicted."

This Amendment is gone altogether since President Obama signed into law a bill that lets the government imprison American Citizens deemed to be a possible combatant without Bail or Trial forever if they want. On December 31, 2011, President Barack Obama signed the National Defense Authorization Act, NDAA, that was ratified in 2013 when it passed the Senate with a 98-0 vote. The authorization gave the government the ability to be able to detain American Citizens without a trial indefinitely, eliminating habeas corpus for the American people.

The Ninth Amendment:

"The enumeration in the Constitution, of certain rights, shall not be construed to deny or disparage others retained by the people."

The Ninth Amendment was supposed to give Rights you never knew you had. But it too has been ignored by the government, and since few people know about the Ninth

Amendment, which reaffirms in pretty broad terms the rights "retained by the people"; Those in power have pretend that it really doesn't exist. The right to die, or what you can do to or with your own body, and the right to do whatever you want with your own property were "Unremunerated" Rights including, the right to privacy The Founding Fathers were trying to acknowledge some of the rights that no government could deny free people. But of course that didn't stop the government from denying freedom to all the people.

The Tenth Amendment:

"The powers not delegated to the United States by the Constitution, nor prohibited by it to the States, are reserved to the States respectively, or to the people."

Well of course this is another Right ignored and abused. Wikipedia sums it up: "The Tenth Amendment is similar to an earlier provision of the Articles of Confederation: "Each state retains its sovereignty, freedom, and independence, and every power, jurisdiction, and right, which is not by this Confederation expressly delegated to the United States, in Congress assembled." After the Constitution was ratified, some wanted to add a similar amendment limiting the federal government to powers "expressly" delegated, which would have denied implied powers. However, the word "expressly" ultimately did not appear in the Tenth Amendment as ratified, and therefore the Tenth Amendment did not reject the powers implied by the Necessary and Proper Clause."

When James Madison introduced the Tenth Amendment in Congress, he explained that many states were eager to ratify this amendment, despite critics who deemed the amendment superfluous or unnecessary: *"I find, from looking into the amendments proposed by the State conventions, that several are particularly anxious that it should be declared in the Constitution, that the powers not therein delegated should be reserved to the several States. Perhaps words which may define this more precisely than the whole of the instrument now does, may be considered as superfluous. I admit they may be deemed unnecessary: but there can be no harm in making such a declaration, if gentlemen will allow that the fact is as stated. I am sure I understand it so, and do therefore propose it"- James Madison.*

I think it's interesting to note that the 1st, 2nd, 4th, 5th, 6th, 8th, 9th, and 10th Amendments were originally shred by President (Honest Abe) Lincoln during the Civil War. One of the great things he is known for is freeing the black slaves, but he unwittingly then helped enslave us all, by deliberately ignoring parts of Constitution that got in his way and set the precedent for future presidents to further shred the Bill of Rights.

Honest Abe was given his name facetiously by people who really knew his two faced side, in the same way the biggest kid in school is called tiny. Honest Abe threatened anyone who invoked the Constitution during the Civil War. A classic example is the threats that were aimed at former President Franklin Pierce by the Lincoln Administration, when President Pierce denounced Lincoln for ignoring the Constitutional Rights and the people of the States. Lincoln basically told Pierce he better stop or else, meaning Lincoln would charge him with treason. But former President Pierce ignored the threats and kept on sighting the Constitution as the foundation of Freedom in the U.S.

From Lincoln on, just about every President since has ignored parts of the Constitution that got in their way. Now the original 10 Amendments of the Constitutional Bill of Rights have little meaning or respect by our Government or the complacent and apathetic American people. It is no longer the Land of the Free and Home of the Brave. It has become the Land of the Few Free and Home of the Humble.

***

Chapter Four

Seeing Through Corporate Control and America's Apathetic Complacency

I don't know what it's going to take to get people to understand that our freedom is in jeopardy if we all don't demand that the government comply with the Constitution. But I do know if we cannot get people to realize this and take a stand, then the very real threat of losing all freedom in this country is imminent and America will lose its status as being the freest nation very soon, if it already hasn't!

I realize people like myself are really up against a major propaganda machine with a media that has become nothing more than a stenographer for corporate government propaganda. Most people don't want to hear how their freedom is slipping away. I see people who just refuse to believe the government would deliberately do anything against the people. Even after seeing the NDAA passed by the federal government, Wikileaks, and the information Edward Snowden released that prove beyond a shadow of doubt that our government has been Unconstitutionally spying, arresting, killing and bold faced lying to us! Through all of this the majority of the populace stand by apathetic and complacent. It reminds me of the HG Wells "Time Machine" movie version with Rod Taylor, where the people of the future watch a girl "Weena" I believe her name was, fall into a river and start to drown, and no one lifts a hand to help. No one but Rod Taylor even cared or showed any emotional response. Have we as a Nation really become so cold and uncaring about our future and freedom? Or have we just become too afraid to say or do anything about it?

Our Government is threatening Reporters, Elected Officials, Military Personnel, Public Employees, and even Us, if we expose their illegal actions against our American Rights, and most of the people don't seem to realize how serious this really is… It's absolutely amazing to me!

The Militarization of the Police

America is beginning to see its police force turned into a military force right in front of their eyes. Military Armored vehicles, military uniforms and military weapons are replacing the men in Blue and it's transforming our country into a national army at an alarming rate. Anyone who can say with a straight face that this is a great model for a Free Country needs to have their head examined or needs to be deprogrammed.

What this should tell the American people is that our government is preparing for the use of deadly force against us; Just incase we ever wake up one day and realize that they are way out of control; and we decide to stand up for ourselves and attempt to put that evil government genie back into its proverbial bottle.

But where are our elected representatives in all of this militarization? Why aren't we hearing them denounce this national build up of military troops in our country? Could they be a part of this, or could they be too scared and threatened by a government machine that they can't even control? Why are they going along with recommendations by police and sheriffs to buy military equipment like armored trucks and gun tanks? Do you know how easy it would be to install a chaingun or a 50 or 75 caliber rapid fire weapon to the tanks? Pretty easy since everything is there but the guns. These tanks and armored gun trucks can blow through block walls and go through your homes and cars like they are tissue paper.

DHS BUYS 2500 ARMORED FIGHTING VEHICLES
Government Plans For War With American Citizens

We really need to ask a couple questions like: How much does the government really know about the pending financial collapse that many of our financial advisors are predicting? Do they have any intention of telling us about it or when they expect it to happen? From the military build up in our communities it would seem they expect this to happen soon. We have to look at this from a financial perspective, because if this country was in the black and everyone was working and making money, there wouldn't be any need for Tanks and Machine Guns in the hands of the Police. So things must be coming to a head pretty soon, as many financial pundits are predicting. This Country can not keep shelling out billions a day it does not have to pay its bills without either having a plan to deal with it the day it all comes crashing down, or foreseeing a turn-around coming in the very near future. I for one do not see that turn around happening anytime soon, but one can always hope.

One of the most concerning parts of this military build-up of our police is the cost. If the government just stopped spending money we don't have, we could avoid a financial collapse; But since our government is the largest employer in the country, cutting spending would also cut jobs which would add to civil unrest and the government might need the military to crush any civil unrest. A very real conundrum indeed. Crimes like theft and robbery are on the rise because of the unemployment problem in America, so they don't want to make it worse. Yet we see and allow our government officials to side with the socialists, tree-huggers and climate doomsdayers and regulate business out of this country. They full well know it is only a matter of time before it all comes crashing down and people hit the streets in protest. So they also have to know the people will be gunned down by the very people who are supposed to protect and serve.

To make matters worse we have a President and Senate bent on taxing the people into bankruptcy with absurd taxations like ObamaCare when they have exempted themselves from being forced to buy it. The commoners in America will be attacked by the IRS (a proven rogue discriminatory agency) with a threat of fines and or imprisonment, if they say No Way to Obama Care and refuse to buy Health Insurance from a Private Company... Seriously do you call this Freedom? The majority of the states and people do not want Obama Care, but they do little to stop it. Is this because of apathy, complacency, fear, or that we just don't know what to do? Are we feeling overwhelmed and overcome by our government? Well we can do something by starting with our local government.

This all starts at the local level, because we have control over our City Council and County Supervisor. If we complain about the Militarizing of our police and sheriff, or some state or federal law that we want them to publicly denounce and they ignore us, then recall is in order, or we can wait and vote them out when they come up for re-election. We should and can make it clear to who ever we elect that we want to get rid of the military police force and return to community policing where they have cops that walk a beat. This is good healthy policing literally!

Environmental Scares

Water has also started to become a controlling factor. Our government knows water is something this planet can not live without, so we are starting to see them use this valuable resource as another way to control us. They know when they have control of our water, they have control our life! We are hearing the media tell us we have a water crisis and we must conserve water. Don't believe it for a moment, it is just the beginning of their brainwash propaganda. Think for yourselves when you see all these Hollywood stars and commentators tell us there is a water shortage across the planet, and then look at all the flooding that has happened that year. They will show a drought in places in America that didn't have a water problem years ago, but what they won't tell us is that area is having a drought because the environmentalists had the dams removed to protect a tiny guppy that they thought was impacted by the dam that had been there for 75 years. If America is having a water shortage it's because we aren't building enough dams and canals for storing the abundant amount of water that floods and destroys communities each year. It is all about who controls the water, plain and simple.

Once we get duped into believing the lies that those in power feed us about an illusionary water problem, and we don't challenge them, we all lose. Because once they get total control of the water, game over!

It all comes down to dollars and cents, and that means controlling us. Most every new law the government creates that is suppose to protect us cost us more of our freedom. It is merely an illusion to make us feel protected, when all the while they have an agenda, controlling us completely. Just as if we are a pet or farm animal, because we are a Cash-Cow to our government and just like any farm animal, we are expected to earn our keep or off to the chopping block we go! This is NOT what our Founding Fathers had in mind when they created this country, they expected us to manage the government and control it, not the other way around!

Years ago people who were self-sufficient and grew their own food, raised their own livestock, created their own energy and didn't need to buy much from anyone, were people we admired. Now they are hated and called isolationists and un-american and even tax evaders because they don't make an income and they don't need to. They grow, raise, or make most everything they need and try to stockpile whatever they can't use right away. The only thing self-sufficient folks can't get around is property tax. Property tax was put in place for the reason stated above. The government has a hard time getting any revenue out of people who are self-sufficient.

The government relies on our need to buy new cars, homes, computers, health insurance, car insurance, home owners insurance, DMV fees and many other government revenue generating things that they can collect tax on, so they can stay in power. Everytime you buy something other than most food what do you have to pay extra? Tax! If you are in the business of selling things, what do you have to pay on the money you make? Tax! What do you get taken out of your hard earned 40 hour paycheck? Tax! Even if you are on unemployment or disability you are Taxed. The government pretty much has their hand in everything!

It's only a matter of time before all food items will have some kind of tax or environmental fee attached to it. And I doubt anyone will say or do anything about it, because at first it will be associated with an environmental problem and only be a cent or two on the dollar. Then inch by inch and year by year the need to increase the tax and or fee will rise. It's the classic frog in the pot syndrome, where you place a frog in a pot of cold water and slowly turn up the heat. The frog does not realize what is happening until it is too late, and unfortunately if we keep going at the rate we've been going for the last 30 years or so, and we don't put a stop to this; It won't be too long before we can't jump out of that pot of boiling water and our future and the future of our children will be cooked.

Social Economic Engineering

We have been herded into a consumption society expected to buy, buy, buy and spend, spend, spend, so the government can Tax, Tax, Tax, us to support themselves. It isn't working though, because it can't ever keep up with the spending promises the government has made. And like any pyramid scheme, it one day will come crashing down and only those at the top of the pyramid are the winners because they got theirs already.

Social Economic Engineering has been around since the government has been taxing, but it really took center stage in the 1970s. The new version relies on fast moving technology to provide the public stimulus to work now. Social Economic Engineering, is the art of manipulating people into performing actions, i.e. buying or spending or believing something. It's a type of confidence trick for the purpose of information gathering, fraud, or manipulating people to buy into a scheme. It differs a little from traditional Social Engineering cons, that often is a mere step in a more complex fraud scheme, by using statistics to brainwash people into believing there is no scheme, and their skewed statistics prove their weak or totally bogus claims.

Wikipeda.org sums up "Social engineering" as "An act of psychological manipulation, that had previously been associated with the social sciences, but its usage has caught on among computer and information security professionals." This includes the State and Federal Governments. What this does is utilize information gathered to be used to manipulate people into believing some issue or some product is either good or bad. The Government controls the Media and has been using this technique for a long time to make us believe something, by using supposed factual information gathered by social engineers...it's even been used in Hollywood programs and movies to control how we think. Yes, I know this is a little hard to wrap your head around, but I guess the easiest way to explain this is, Subliminal Perception Messaging, anything that sends you a message without your Conscious Knowledge of it, usually picked up by your subconscious mind, or in short; Mind

Control normally using an emotional stimuli. We have been, and still are, being mentally conditioned to believe whatever those in control want us to believe, and unless we can see through the manipulation, or know what is being told to us is a bold faced lie, we don't have a clue to what is really going on and will tend to believe it.

Unfortunately too many people are way too gullible and believe many of the untrue stories they are told. If we are told a lie over and over again we start to believe it. There is a saying that if you tell a lie three or more times in the media people will tend to believe it, even the people in the media who are telling the lie start to believe it themselves. Social Economic Engineering is not much different with the exception that it uses supposed data and statistics to back up weak claims or down right untrue claims. Mark Twain pretty much hit the nail on the head when he said; *"There are three kinds of lies...Lies, damned lies, and statistics".* Obama Care comes to mind, doesn't it?

The US Department of Commerce has even gotten into the act and in 2013 started using the US Census Bureau to knock on doors and ask residents if they were victims of crime. Although this letter states in the third paragraph it is voluntary now, you can bet it will become mandatory in the future. Notice how official it looks and if you merely glance over it like most people will do, or you don't even bother to read it, you can get the impression that it's mandatory that you answer the questions when the census worker comes to your door. Once people except this it will become mandatory, and you can bet your life and carve it in stone that they will in the future be asking each house member if they have guns in the home. The data gathered clearly states in this letter that it will be used by legislators and policy makers so watch out America, and get ready for more laws backed up by statistics that the government has setup to skew a subject like gun control, because this clever deception is just another form of Social Engineering.

Social Security and especially ObamaCare is another example of agencies that uses social engineering and deception to gain information from those who collect it, but I will save those Ponzi Schemes for my next book.

UNITED STATES DEPARTMENT OF COMMERCE
Economics and Statistics Administration
U.S. Census Bureau
Washington, DC 20233-0001
OFFICE OF THE DIRECTOR

FROM THE DIRECTOR
U.S. CENSUS BUREAU

The U.S. Census Bureau is conducting a survey for the U.S. Department of Justice to obtain information on the type and amount of crime committed against households and individuals throughout the country. A Census Bureau representative will be contacting you soon. Our representative will show an official identification card and ask for some important information on this subject from you and your household.

The information you provide our representative will help inform the country about how much crime there is, where it occurs, when it occurs, what crime costs victims, and which segments of the population are most frequently victimized. Since many crimes are never reported to the police, information from this survey will show a more complete picture of the amount and types of crime occurring in the United States. The survey results are used in many ways, including by citizens to evaluate their vulnerabilities, by legislators and policymakers to develop programs to aid crime victims and prevent crime, and by researchers to understand various aspects of crime victimization.

Your address is part of a scientifically selected sample of addresses chosen throughout the country for participation in this survey. Because this is a sample survey, your answers represent not only you and your household, but also hundreds of other households like yours. For this reason, your voluntary cooperation is very important. I hope you will answer all the survey questions as completely and accurately as possible. Although there are no penalties for failure to answer any questions, each unanswered question substantially lessens the accuracy of the final data. Your answers will be used only to prepare statistical summaries, and no information about your household or you as an individual can be identified from these statistics. The law completely protects your confidential answers from disclosure.

Answers to the most frequently asked survey questions are on the reverse side of this letter. If you would like further information, contact the Census Bureau by writing or calling the following office:

REGIONAL DIRECTOR
US CENSUS BUREAU
15350 SHERMAN WAY STE 400
VAN NUYS CA 91406-4203

Telephone: 1–800–992–3530

Thank you for your cooperation. The Census Bureau appreciates your help.

A Message From the Director

America's Food Poisoning by Government Mandate and Corporate Greed

The Government control over food is just as bad as their attempt to control all the water. Regulation after regulation and law after law are heaped on to, not only the farm and ranch industry, but also the individual citizen who wants to eat Fresh Foods. Police and FDA agents have raided small farms and families for selling milk, cheese, garden vegetables, lemonade and meat, to neighbors who want untainted fresh food. The totally unconstitutional raids were for no other reason than they didn't have government approval, and didn't raise or grow what they sold according to government regulations. The people who were raided weren't alone, no sir, the people who bought from the farmers were also arrested! The farmers had grown and raised their vegetables and animals naturally without any preservatives like most farmers and ranchers used to raise and grow the food that we ate years ago. But because the farmers would dare sell fresh untainted food to their neighbors who had asked them if they could buy it, the government attacks them. I can sight several headline cases such as: "*Wisconsin Farmer to Stand Trial for Selling Raw Milk*" another "*Feds sting Amish farmer selling raw milk*" and on Aug 3, 2011 – "*Police Seize*

Cash, Produce, Dump Raw Milk .... Government arrest and persecute individuals merely for buying and selling raw milk and cheese ... Healthy Family Farms is a sustainable, pasture-based farming operation" ... even children have been arrested for selling Lemonade: *Aug 20, 2011 ... Children Arrested for Selling Lemonade at Capitol... The children were selling lemonade on the Capitol lawn.* The list of attacks by the government on farmers and people who just want to raise, grow and eat fresh natural food goes on and on.

I don't know about some of you younger readers, but I think many of you people 50 and over would agree with me when I say that meat, fish, bird, and vegetables you buy in the supermarket today taste different than it used to taste when you were a kid. I can remember sitting down at the table to a great tasting hamburger and/ or T-bone steak and the roasts my mom used to bake in the 60s were out of this world. Even chicken, turkey and fish just does not taste the same. Food used to taste so much fresher years ago. Back as early as the 1980's you could still get a pretty good piece of beef. Now it seems that you really have to shop around to find any type of food that even comes close to the taste of food years ago. Unless it is from a family farm!

I asked a butcher a while back, why our food does not taste as good as it use to years ago? He told me that most of the farmers of today feed and fertilize with so many chemicals that it is a wonder people are not dropping dead in droves. He told me he was lucky to have a small farm where he could grow and raise his own food like most of the commercial farmers and ranchers used to do back in the 50s and 60s. Food was natural and full of flavor back then, the way it was suppose to be! I recently found out first hand what the butcher told me was true. My daughter and Son-in-law who live on a ranch, butchered one of their cattle and gave my wife and I some of the meat. There was that taste I had been missing! It was the flavor that I remembered years ago that use to make me run to the dinner table. The flavor that I once took for granted.

They allow their cattle to graze in the spring through fall and feed them grain and cattle feed in the winter. No anti-bodies or other chemicals are ingested by the cattle. They do not use chemical fertilizers on the pasture, just good old natural horse manure and boy does it show by the taste of the beef! Grass and other grain really grow good with just plain old natural fertilizer, no pesticides or chemicals just manure. But that wasn't the only surprise I had over what fresh good tasting food really used to taste like. Several weeks before my daughter had bestowed that prized beef on me, my young grandson Alec had gone fishing in Alaska with his other grandpa and brought back some fresh Ocean Halibut and Salmon that they had caught. Once again I tasted fish like it used to taste, fresh! Not "Farm Raised" or whatever they sell in the supermarkets today.

Sadly, since government regulations have become so expensive for farmers and ranchers, many of them have just quit. Now only the large corporate government controlled farmers and ranchers are supplying the stores with chemically enriched produce, poultry, Sea food and beef; which the large chemical corporations with government contracts control. If the little farmers attempts to sell, or even in some cases, give what they grow and raise to anyone other than their family, without all the permits, licenses and regulations required...off to jail they go... Another freedom lost...I don't believe for a moment this is good for America's Health, do you?

Let's look at America's health from the late 1960s to today, and the government regulations the FDA passed on farming and ranching from the same time. This information is readily available to anyone on the internet. The chemicals listed below have been introduced in our food for about 40 years now.

Bovine Growth Hormone (rBGH)

This genetically modified hormone was developed to be injected into dairy cows to produce more milk. Cows subjected to rBGH suffer excruciating pain due to swollen udders and mastitis, and the pus from the resulting infection enters the milk supply requiring the use of additional antibiotics. rBGH milk has been linked to breast cancer, colon cancer, and prostate cancer in humans. Bovine somatotropin or bovine somatotrophin (abbreviated bST and BST), or BGH, is a peptide hormone produced by a cow's pituitary gland. Like other hormones, it is produced in small quantities and is used in regulating metabolic processes. After the biotech company Genentech discovered and patented the gene for BST in the 1970s, it became possible to synthesize the hormone using recombinant DNA technology to create recombinant bovine somatotropin (rBST), recombinant bovine growth hormone (rBGH), or artificial growth hormone. Four large pharmaceutical companies, Monsanto, American Cyanamid, Eli Lilly, and Upjohn, developed commercial rBST products and submitted them to the US Food and Drug Administration (FDA) for approval and rBST was approved for use.

Genetically Modified Crops, (GMOs)

In the 1980s and early 1990s, began gene-splicing corn, cotton, soy, and canola with DNA from a foreign source to achieve a couple of traits; an internally generated pesticide and an internal resistance to the weed killers like Round-Up so farmers could control weeds without hurting the crop. Despite decades of promises that genetically engineered crops would feed the world with more nutrients, that were drought resistant and had greater yield, the GMO crops haven't lived up to the promise. They have however, caused health problems, according to the Organic Consumers Association, *"There is a direct correlation between our genetically engineered food supply and the $2 trillion the U.S. spends annually on medical care, namely an epidemic of diet-related chronic diseases."*

The U.S. government subsidizes corporate farms and food processors that produce genetically engineered junk food that has increased heart disease, stroke, diabetes and cancers. You would think the US Government would be supporting naturally grown healthy fruits, vegetables, grains, and range and pasture fed animals, but most organic farmers receive no such subsidies and are often targeted by the FDA. Why? Could it be that naturally grown food means no money for the government and the chemical corporations who support the government with taxes and their contribution/pay-offs?

Unfortunately most of the land we grow food on has already been chemically altered and it can take years for some of the chemicals to degrade. Take the Rice Growing industry for instance. Before 2000 most Rice Farmers would burn their fields to control pests and disease, but after 2000 regulations were put on burning, chemicals were used instead. A lot of old style ways of farming have been forgotten or made illegal and farmers are left with little choice but to use chemicals. One drawback to all this chemical use is human occupational exposure to pesticides and chemicals that has become a significant cause of death.

Ask yourself, is the government mandates on food and their seemingly deliberate attacks on people who wish to eat naturally good for America's Health and our Freedom? Or is this just another illusion of control. I think another question should be asked; who is profiting from these mandates and laws? Remember, everything you buy has a tax attached to it somewhere down the line, either a sales tax or an income tax or both.

Corporate Government

It's hard for most people to believe they have no control over their lives and their government. Hopefully some of the things you have just read in the previous chapters are starting to tie things altogether. The real controllers of the government today are corporations and money. Our founding fathers knew this all too well and attempted to put the long ignored checks and balances in the Constitution. Corporations like the East Indies Company, that traded mainly in cotton, silk, indigo dye, salt, saltpeter, tea and opium. The Company was granted a Royal Charter by Queen Elizabeth in 1600, making it the oldest among several similarly formed European East India Companies. Shares of the company were owned by wealthy merchants and aristocrats, many of whom had ties to the government. The government owned no shares and had only indirect control. The Company eventually came to rule large areas of India with its own private armies, exercising military power and assuming administrative functions. It also had major influence on the British Government, just as many corporations today have major influence on the government.

Most media is corporate driven, meaning the corporation controls most of what you see and how you see it. Corporations are great users of social engineering, and even the supposed news media is controlling what you see and read. So the Corporations control the media and the government and you are merely a resource to them. Yet, most people seem content with this and don't really care as long as they have some creature comforts. The mass feed their children poison and teach the children to obey the corporate government, and they do it without thinking of the future consequence, as if they are zombified. Is this what man has to look forward to, mindless compulsion? We should not comply with bad laws and regulations created by ruthless tyrants! Our Constitution and Founding Fathers pretty much demanded it, if we were to remain a Free Nation.

Sadly we have to realize some hard cold facts. One is that we live in a parasitic universe and everything feeds off of something. We also have to understand the two constants in this dimensional universe; Nothing lives or lasts forever and everything must come to an end and die one day. So for us to believe that freedom in the USA will last, is a fallacy... but to believe there is nothing you can do to change the speed at which it ends is also a fallacy. We have the power, and the corporate government not only knows it, but is terrified that we may one day wake up and use that power. This is why we are seeing the build up of military police and the confiscation of weapons and freedom. People like you and I are waking up and saying NO to the powers that be that have been herding us like sheep to the slaughter house. The government and their corporate bosses are preparing for that day when everything comes crashing down and the people decide to band together and march in on them for all the crimes they have committed against humanity and our Constitution. So we must be prepared or we will be caught like a deer in the headlights of an oncoming Tank or armored truck, with a driver that knows they have to speed up to avoid major damage!

****

Chapter 5

Be Prepared for the Worst

We don't have much time left to effectively stop this total takeover of all freedom in America. We have to get all the people to realize they are being manipulated into the classic divide and conquer approach to totally conquering them. We have a major divide in this country which is purposely being fueled to create the Illusion that you need more rules and laws to protect you from the other side. This is going to be the hardest thing to overcome. Hate runs long and deep, and the left vs. right has been played for a long, long time.

Both sides point the finger at each other and say we don't own, watch, read or eat the same thing! So because of this we try and pass a law to stop the other side from owning, watching, reading or eating something different then us. We do this in a fueled anger created by our government even if we have to cut off our own nose to spite our face! All the while, our controllers sit back calm and collect, as they manipulate our feelings and point us in the direction they want us to go.

Who are the controllers you ask? They are a rogue government shadow corporation that have far more power than the President will ever have! They are comprised of people that we will never know or see to our knowledge. They have been in the shadow for as long as time and are the reason and the start of government control. They are very powerful individuals and have been controlling and manipulating us and our government like farm animals for centuries all for revenue generation!

There are two very effective ways to get a person to do or believe something: One is to tell them the truth and hope they believe it and do the right thing. The other is to get them angry or sad at the truth and then point that anger or sadness in the direction that they want it to go. This is called control by using an emotional stimuli and it works really well; especially if the person you are using it on has no idea what you are up to. This is also used openly by Military Law Enforcers who are trained to deliberately push your buttons and get you mad at them or sad over something, so you will do or say something that they can arrest you for, or get information out of you. Watch out for the direct and indirect use of this technique. We have to remember to try and stay in control and not allow ourselves to be controlled or manipulated or we will lose! I know it is hard not to get mad at views you strongly disagree with, and God knows I lose my temper when I am confronted with a person I know is trying to push my buttons. It is really hard not to blow up, especially when you have those people who deliberately try and push you to the breaking point just so they can say; *"Whats the matter with you, why are you freaking out, you are crazy or are you insane!"* This way they can try and destroy any credibility you had and and make you out to look like a nut.

Express Yourself

We need to express our likes and dislikes to our elected representatives. I hear time after time from people that it does not matter what they say, and it does not do any good to call their elected officials because they do not listen. This is another fallacy! They must be listening to someone or they wouldn't vote the way they do on issues that directly affect you. What you have to do to be effective, is talk with your neighbors and friends and see if they feel the same way you do. If they do, write up a letter of approval or disapproval on the subject and have them sign it, get as many signatures as you can and send it in to your local elected official. Then call them after you know they have had time to read it, like three days to a week later. *(You will need to wait a couple of weeks for State and Federal*

Representatives to get around to reading it.) Believe me, they'll be more inclined to listen to you then!

Another very effective way is to gather the people who feel the same way as you do on an issue, and go to the Government meetings. City Council, County Supervisors, School Boards as well as other local agencies have regular monthly and weekly meetings that the public can attend. You can speak out on your concerns at the meetings when they ask if there are any public comments. It is best to call ahead and make it known that you will be there and what the topic is. Then you will be put on the agenda for that meeting and who ever you are going in front of will call you up and make it known to the people what you are there for. You usually will have a time limit, but if you are already on the agenda it does help since they expected you and have set that time aside. Of course it is best to have everything you want to state written down so you can make sure that you get your point across and get all your questions answered. Being a former elected official, I can assure you this will get their attention, and if it doesn't all you need to do is mention the word, "Recall" and that will get their attention for sure.

Get to know your State Reps. I know my assemblyman and have his personal cell phone number. You may not be able to get your State Reps cell number but you sure can speak with their office staff and complain. Now if you really get involved as I have, you can help get your people elected to office and then the odds are that you too might have a personal cell phone number or direct line you can call when you want to express yourself. But if you stand on the sidelines and never get involved, you won't have anyone to call and you will surely lose your freedom!

Civil Disobedience

We are going to see a lot more regulations and laws passed to control us. You may have to break those regulations and laws to regain your freedom. Civil Disobedience has been the most used way to affect change. Wikipedia, the free encyclopedia, describes this as the active, professed refusal to obey certain laws, demands, and commands of a government, or of an occupying international power. Civil disobedience is commonly, though not always, defined as being nonviolent resistance. It is one form of civil resistance. In one view (in India, known as ahimsa or satyagraha) it could be said that it is compassion in the form of respectful disagreement.

Thoureau's 1848 essay called; *"Civil Disobedience"*, was originally titled; "Resistance to Civil Government", has had a wide influence on many later practitioners of civil disobedience. The driving idea behind the essay is that citizens are morally responsible for their support of aggressors, even when such support is required by law. In the essay, Thoreau explained his reasons for having refused to pay taxes as an act of protest against slavery and against the Mexican-American War. He writes; *"If I devote myself to other pursuits and contemplations, I must first see, at least, that I do not pursue them sitting upon another man's shoulders. I must get off him first, that he may pursue his contemplations too. See what gross inconsistency is tolerated. I have heard some of my townsmen say, 'I should like to have them order me out to help put down an insurrection of the slaves, or to march to Mexico; — see if I would go'; and yet*

these very men have each, directly by their allegiance, and so indirectly, at least, by their money, furnished a substitute."

Henry David Thoreau's classic essay *Civil Disobedience* inspired Martin Luther King, Mahatma Gandhi and many other activists.

In seeking an active form of civil disobedience, one may choose to deliberately break certain laws, such as by forming a peaceful blockade or occupying a facility illegally, though sometimes violence has been known to occur, and protesters practice this non-violent form of civil disorder have to have the expectation that they might or will be arrested. You also have to expect that you might be violently attacked by the authorities and maybe even killed. Protesters often undergo training in advance on how to react to arrest or an attack, so that they will do so in a manner that quietly or limply resists without threatening the authorities, so they can avoid getting hurt.

Mahatma Gandhi outlined several rules for civil resisters (or *satyagrahi*) in the time when he was leading India in the struggle for Independence from the British Empire. For instance, they were to express no anger, never retaliate, submit to the opponent's orders and assaults, submit to arrest by the authorities, surrender personal property when confiscated by the authorities but refuse to surrender property held in trust, refrain from swearing and insults (which are contrary to *ahimsa*), refrain from saluting the Union flag, and protect officials from insults and assaults even at the risk of the resister's own life. This worked in India's case but doesn't always work. China is one of those cases where peaceful protest can get you killed.

Now one other effective way of peacefully protesting is to form a general American strike. This has never been effectively acomplished yet, but it would get the attention of the government really fast, especially if it lasted for days or weeks. However, it would take hundreds of millions of people all across the county to be successful. Essentially people would just quit working and quit buying anything so no taxes would be paid which would eventually shut down the country's revenue. We have seen this in mid-eastern countries and it does work, but it takes weeks or even months to bring a country or government to it's knees.

*****

Chapter 6

Recalling Elected Officials

Recalling an official that has lied and or does not listen to the voters can be a challenge. The politicians know it isn't an easy task and most of the time they will lay low or go into PR mode to try and make the unaware public believe that the people that are trying to recall them are crazy or just have some axe to grind. They will attempt to use the media if they can, and if they can't, they just might go directly to the voters in person or by mail. Recall stipulations can vary from state to state so you might want to check on how they work, and what you need to do in your area with your local elections office. Normally you need to get a percentage of the voters to sign the Recall petition. I have a sample of a California Intention to Recall Petition that you will see in this chapter... I wish more people would use it.

What is a Recall and What Circumstances Justify It?

The California Constitution defines a recall as "the power of the electors to remove an elective officer" (Art. II, Sec. 13).

Neither the California Constitution nor the Elections Code states under what circumstances a recall is justified.

Instead, the Constitution states, in connection with the recall of state officers, "sufficiency of reason is not reviewable" (Art. II, Sec. 14). The only language in the Elections Code that has any bearing on this is in (§11024), referring to the proponent's statement of reason for the recall and the officer's answer. It says that, "the statement and answer are intended solely for the information of the voters". No insufficiency in form or substance thereof shall affect the validity of the election proceeding.

Who can be recalled?

Any elective officer, including any officer appointed in lieu of election or to fill a vacancy (§11006).

This may differ in other States so check with your election office.

Circumstances under which a recall is prohibited.

When a person has been appointed to office pursuant to §10229 (because no person has been nominated to office), a recall may not be commenced against an officer if one or more of the following conditions apply (§11007):

• The officer has not held office during his or her current term for more than 90 days.

• A recall election has been decided in the officer's favor within the last six months.

• The officer's term of office ends within six months or less.

Who Conducts the Recall Election?

The county elections official (i.e., the County Clerk or Registrar of Voters) conducts the election in the case of the recall of elective officers of a county, school district, county board of education, community college district, resident voting district and judges of trial courts (§11002).

However, in the event that the county elections official is the officer whose recall is being sought, then the duties imposed upon him or her shall be performed by some other person designated by the Board of Supervisors (§11201).

Who Can Initiate a Recall?

Any qualified elector may initiate a recall. A qualified elector is defined as a registered voter of the jurisdiction who is eligible to vote for the officer. He or she can seek to recall (§§11005 and 322).

So any registered voter in the district can start a recall and collect signatures.

Steps to Initiate a Recall

Each recall is a separate process and requires successful completion of specific steps. Please note that if there are three separate officers to be recalled, then three of each of the following documents must be prepared by the proponent(s) of the recall (§§11021 and 11044):

• Notice of Intention

• Affidavit of Time and Manner of Service

• Affidavit of Proof of Publication (or Posting, if applicable) of the Notice of Intention

• Set of Two Blank Copies of the Proposed Petition Formats

• Recall Petition

Any error or discrepancy in following any of the steps in connection with a particular recall may require that some or all steps taken up to that point be done over. Recall proponents may wish to consult an attorney to help them avoid such errors.

19 States that permit recall of state officials

Alaska, Arizona, California, Colorado, Georgia, Idaho, Illinois, Kansas, Louisiana, Michigan, Minnesota, Montana, Nevada, New Jersey, North Dakota, Oregon, Rhode Island, Washington, and Wisconsin.

When multiple recalls are under way, petition circulators will typically circulate several petitions, and request voters to sign each of however many petitions are involved. Not all voters will choose to sign each petition, meaning that when the petitions are filed with the county elections official, the total number of signatures submitted for each recall petition may vary.

The District of Columbia also allows recalls. Virginia has a process similar to a recall, but it is not listed here as a recall state because its process, while requiring citizen petitions, calls for a recall trial rather than an election. After sufficient petition signatures are gathered and verified, a circuit court decides whether a Virginia official will be removed from office. In all other recall states, the voters decide through an election. In at least 29 states (some sources place this number at 36) recall elections may be held in local jurisdictions.

Petition must be in at least 8-point type, and 8 ½ by 14" paper is recommended. The request for the election, the Notice of Intention and the answer must be printed on each side of the sheet of paper on which signatures appear. All petition sections must be printed in uniform size and darkness with uniform spacing. §11041

Must have 1" top margin

SAMPLE PETITION FOR RECALL

TO THE HONORABLE (*INSERT NAME OF THE GOVERNING BODY THAT CALLS THE ELECTION*)
　　Pursuant to the California Constitution and California Election laws, we the undersigned registered and qualified electors of the (*insert electoral jurisdiction*) of (*insert geographic location*), California respectfully state that we seek the recall and removal of (*insert name of person whose recall is being sought*) holding the office of (*insert name of office*) in (*insert electoral jurisdiction*), California.
　　We demand an election of a successor to that office.
　　The following Notice of Intention to Circulate Recall Petition was served on (*insert date petition was served*) to (*insert name of person whose recall is being sought*).

NOTICE OF INTENTION TO CIRCULATE RECALL PETITION

TO THE HONORABLE (*INSERT NAME OF THE PUBLIC OFFICIAL WHOSE RECALL IS BEING SOUGHT*),
　　Pursuant to Section 11020 of the California Elections Code, the undersigned, registered qualified voters of the (*insert name of district*), County of (*insert name of county*), State of California, hereby give notice that we are the proponents of a recall petition and that we intend to seek your recall and removal from the office of (*insert title of office*), in the (*insert name of district*), County of (*insert name of county*), State of California, and to demand an election of a successor for that office.

The grounds for the proposed recall are as follows:

(*Insert grounds for the recall*)

The printed names, signatures, and business or residence addresses of the proponents are as follows:
(*Insert names, addresses, and "s/name of voter" for signature.*)

When printing the Notice of Intention (200 words or less) on the petition, it must appear exactly as written on the original Notice, including punctuation, spelling, etc. and it must contain the names of at least 10 recall proponents. It may differ from the original Notice in the following ways:
1. it does not have to contain more than 10 names, even if a larger number was required on the original notice;
2. the business or residence addresses of the proponents may be omitted. If so, revise the statement appearing before the signatures to read: "The names of the proponents (business or residence addresses are on file with the elections official) are as follows:"
3. it does not have to include the paragraph regarding the incumbent's right to file an answer.

The answer of the officer sought to be recalled is as follows:
(*insert answer here*)

Insert answer – 200 words. If no answer, insert "No Answer was Filed." §11041 (a) (3)

Each of the undersigned states for himself/herself that he or she is a registered and qualified elector of (*insert electoral jurisdiction*) of (*insert geographic location*), California.

	PRINT YOUR NAME	RESIDENCE ADDRESS ONLY	FOR OFFICIAL USE ONLY
1.			1" column §11043(c)
	YOUR SIGNATURE	CITY　　ZIP	
2.	PRINT YOUR NAME	RESIDENCE ADDRESS ONLY	
	YOUR SIGNATURE	CITY　　ZIP	
3.	PRINT YOUR NAME	RESIDENCE ADDRESS ONLY	
	YOUR SIGNATURE	CITY　　ZIP	
4.	PRINT YOUR NAME	RESIDENCE ADDRESS ONLY	
	YOUR SIGNATURE	CITY　　ZIP	

This declaration below may be omitted on front side if signature spaces are provided on both sides. The circulator's declaration must follow the last signature block. All other information above must be included on both sides.

DECLARATION OF PERSON CIRCULATING SECTION OF RECALL PETITION
(MUST BE IN CIRCULATOR'S OWN HANDWRITING)

I _____ , declare:
(Print Name)

1. My residence address is _____ , in _____
(Street Address)　　　　(City)　　　　(County)
County, California, and I am a registered voter in (*insert electoral jurisdiction*);

2. I personally circulated the attached petition for signing.

3. I witnessed each of the appended signatures being written on the petition and to my best information and belief, each signature is the genuine signature of the person whose name it purports to be; and

4. The appended signatures were obtained between the dates of _____ and _____ , inclusive.
(Starting Date)　　　　(Ending Date)
I declare under penalty of perjury under the laws of the State of California that the foregoing is true and correct.

Executed on _____ at _____ , California.
(Date)　　　　(City or Community Where Signed)

Petition must have ½ inch margin on bottom. §11043(b)

_____
(Signature)

You may insert a return address and deadline here.

(Note: Federal officeholders are not subject to recall.)

Elected Officials Who Have Been Through Recall Since 1913:

1913: **California** state senator Marshall Black was recalled.

1914: **California** state senator Edwin Grant was recalled.

1914: **California** state senator James Owens survived a recall election.

1921: **North Dakota** Governor Lynn Joseph Frazier was recalled.

1932: **Wisconsin** state senator Otto Mueller survived a recall election.

1935: **Oregon** state representative Harry Merriam was recalled.

1971: **Idaho** state senator Fisher Ellsworth was recalled.

1971: **Idaho** state representative Aden Hyde was recalled.

1981: **Washington** state senator Peter von Reichbauer survived a recall election.

1983: **Michigan** state senator Phil Mastin was recalled.

1983: **Michigan** state senator David Serotkin was recalled. (Technically he resigned from office before the results of the recall election were certified, but the results were sufficient to recall him.)

1985: **Oregon** state representative Pat Gillis was recalled.

1988: **Oregon** state senator Bill Olson was recalled.

1990: **Wisconsin** state assembly member Jim Holperin survived a recall election.

1994: **California** state senator David Roberti survived a recall election.

1995: **California** assembly member Paul Horcher was recalled.

1995: **California** assembly member Michael Machado survived a recall election.

1995: **California** assembly member Doris Allen was recalled.

1996: **Wisconsin** state senator George Petak was recalled.

2003: **California** Governor Grey Davis was recalled.

2003: **Wisconsin** state senator Gary George was recalled.

2008: **California** state senator Jeff Denham survived a recall election.

2008: **Michigan** house speaker Andy Dillon survived a recall election.

2011: **Wisconsin** state senators Robert Cowles, Alberta Darling, Dave Hansen, Sheila Harsdorf, Jim Holperin, Luther Olsen and Robert Wirch survived attempted recalls, while Senators Randy Hopper and Dan Kapanke were recalled.

2011: **Arizona** Senate President Russell Pearce was recalled on November 8.

2011: **Michigan** state representative Paul Scott was recalled on November 8.

2012: **Wisconsin** state senator Van Wanggaard was recalled. Senate Republican leader Scott Fitzgerald and Senator Terry Moulton survived recall elections. Senator Pam Galloway resigned earlier in the year when sufficient signatures were gathered to trigger a recall election. Even though her name wasn't on the ballot, a recall election was still held for her seat. All four senate seats in the recall election were held by Republicans; after the recall, three remain in Republican hands and one switched to the Democrats, giving control of the Senate to the Democratic Party.

2013: **Colorado** Senate President John Morse and Senator Angela Giron were recall on September 10, 2013 because of their support for very strict anti-Second Amendment gun control laws in Colorado.

Specific grounds for recall are required in only eight states:

Grounds for Recall

Alaska: Lack of fitness, incompetence, neglect of duties or corruption (AS §15.45.510)

Georgia: Act of malfeasance or misconduct while in office; violation of oath of office; failure to perform duties prescribed by law; willfully misused, converted, or misappropriated, without authority, public property or public funds entrusted to or associated with the elective office to which the official has been elected or appointed. Discretionary performance of a lawful act or a prescribed duty shall not constitute a ground for recall of an elected public official. (Ga. Code §21-4-3(7) and 21-4-4(c))

Kansas: Conviction for a felony, misconduct in office, incompetence, or failure to perform duties prescribed by law. No recall submitted to the voters shall be held void because of the insufficiency of the grounds, application, or petition by which the submission was procured. (KS Stat. §25-4301)

Minnesota: Serious malfeasance or nonfeasance during the term of office in the performance of the duties of the office or conviction during the term of office of a serious crime (Const. Art. VIII §6)

Montana: Physical or mental lack of fitness, incompetence, violation of oath of office, official misconduct, conviction of certain felony offenses (enumerated in Title 45). No person may be recalled for performing a mandatory duty of the office he holds or for not performing any act that, if performed, would subject him to prosecution for official misconduct. (Mont. Code §2-16-603)

Rhode Island: Authorized in the case of a general officer who has been indicted or informed against for a felony, convicted of a misdemeanor, or against whom a finding of probable cause of violation of the code of ethics has been made by the ethics commission (Const. Art. IV §1)

Virginia: Neglect of duty, misuse of office, or incompetence in the performance of duties when that neglect of duty, misuse of office, or incompetence in the performance of duties has a material adverse effect upon the conduct of the office, or upon conviction of a drug-related misdemeanor or a misdemeanor involving a "hate crime" (§24.2-233)

Washington: Commission of some act or acts of malfeasance or misfeasance while in office, or who has violation of oath of office (Const. Art. I §33)

Source: National Conference of State Legislatures, July 2011

The recall process is similar to the initiative process in that citizen petitions are required. The number of signatures necessary to qualify a recall petition, however, it is often significantly higher than for initiatives. Signature requirements are based on a formula, generally a percentage of the vote in the last election for the office in question, although some states base the formula on the number of eligible voters or other variants. Whatever the formula, the signature requirements are high: 25 percent in nine states; 25 percent for statewide offices and 35 percent for legislators in Washington; one-third in Louisiana; and 40 percent in Kansas. California's requirements are 12 percent for statewide offices; 20 percent for legislators and appellate judges. Georgia requires 15 percent for statewide offices and 30 percent for all others. Idaho requires 20 percent for all offices. Montana has the lowest number of required signatures: 10 percent for statewide officials and 15 percent for state district offices such as legislative districts.

States	Who Can Be Recalled	Signature Requirement	Circulation Time

Alaska	All elected public officers of the state except judicial officers	25% of the votes cast in the last election for the official being recalled	Not specified
Arizona	Every public officer in the state holding an elective office	25% of the votes cast in the last election for the official being recalled	120 days
California	State officers, members of the legislature, judges of courts of appeal	*For statewide officers*: 12% of the votes cast in the last election for the official being recalled, 1% from each of 5 counties *State Senators, members of the Assembly, members of the Board of Equalization, judges of courts of appeal*: 20% of the votes cast in the last election for the official being recalled.	160 days
Colorado	Every elective officer of the state.	25% of the votes cast in the last election for the official being recalled.	60 days

Georgia	Public officials who hold elective office	*For statewide officers*: 15% of eligible voters for office at time of last election, 1/5 from each congressional district *Others*: 30% of eligible voters for office at time of last election	90 days
Idaho	Every public officer in the state except judicial officers.	20% of eligible voters for office at time of last election.	60 days
Illinois	Governor	15% of the votes cast for governor in the preceding general election from each of at least 25 counties. Also required are the signatures from at least 20 members of the House of Representatives and 10 members of the Senate, with no more than half the signatures of	150 days

		members of each chamber from the same political party.	
Kansas	All elected public officers in the state except judicial officers	40% of the votes cast in the last election for the official being recalled	90 days
Louisiana	Any state official except judges of the courts of record	*If over 1,000 eligible voters*: 33.3% of eligible voters for office at time of last election *If fewer than 1,000 eligible voters:* 40% of eligible voters for office at time of last election	180 days
Michigan	All elective officers except judges of the courts of record	25% of total votes cast for position at last election	90 days
Minnesota	State executive officers, legislators, and judges of the supreme court,	25% of total votes cast for position at last election	90 days

	court of appeals or a district court		
Montana	Any person holding a public office of the state	*For statewide officers*: 10% of eligible voters for office at time of last election *For district officers:* 15% of eligible voters for office at time of last election	3 months
Nevada	Every public officer in the state	25% of the votes cast in the last election for the official being recalled	60 days
New Jersey	Any elected official in the state or representing the state in the U.S. Congress	25% of the registered voters in the electoral district of the official sought to be recalled	*Governor or U.S. Senator:* 320 days *All others:* 160 days
North Dakota	Any elected official of the state or legislative district	25% of the votes cast in the last election for the official being recalled	Not specified
Oregon	Every public officer in the	15% of total votes cast in officer's district for	90 days

	state	all candidates for governor in the last election	
Rhode Island	Governor, Lt. Governor, Secretary of State, Treasurer, Attorney General	15% of total votes cast for said office in last general election	90 days
Washington	Every elective public officer of the state except judges of courts of record	*For statewide officers*: 25% of the votes cast in the last election for the official being recalled *Others:* 35% of the votes cast in the last election for the official being recalled	*Statewide officers:* 270 days *Others:* 180 days
Wisconsin	Any state, judicial, congressional or legislative official	25% of total votes cast for the office of governor at the last election within the same district or territory of that officer being recalled	60 days

Source: National Conference of State Legislatures, July 2011

Recall Provisions in State Constitutions and Statutes

Alaska – Const. Art. 11, §8; AS §15.45.510-710, 15.60.010, 29.26.250-350

Arizona - Const. Art. 8, §1-6; Ariz. Rev. Stat. §19-201 – 19-234

California – Const. Art. 2, §13-19; CA Election Code §11000-11386

Colorado – Const. Art. 21; Colo. Rev. Stat. §1-12-101 – 1-12-122, 23-17-120.5, 31-4-501 – 31-4-505

Georgia – Const. Art. 2, §2.4; Ga. Code §21-4-1 et seq.

Idaho – Const. Art. 6, §6; Idaho Code §34-1701 – 34-1715

Illinois - Const. Art. 3. §7

Kansas – Const. Art. 4, §3; KSA §25-4301 – 25-4331

Louisiana – Const. Art. 10, §26; La. Stats. Ann. §18:1300.1 – 18:1300.17

Michigan – Const. Art. 2, §8; Mich. Election Law §168.951 – 168.975

Minnesota – Const. Art. 8, §6; Minn. Stat. Ann. §211C.01 et seq.

Montana – Mont. Code § 2-16-601 – 2-16-635

Nevada – Const. Art. 2, §9; Nev. Rev. Stat. §294A.006, Ch. 306, 539.163 – 539.183

New Jersey – Const. Art. 1, §2(b); NJ Rev. Stat. Ann. § 19:27A-1 – 19:27A-18

North Dakota – Const. Art. 3, §1 and 10; ND Century Code Ann. §16.1-01-09.1, 44-08-21

Oregon – Const. Art. 2, §18; Or. Rev. Stat. §249.865 – 249.880

Rhode Island – Const. Art. 4, §1

Virginia - Va. Code §24.2-233

Washington – Const. Art. 1, Sec. 33-34; Wash. Rev. Code §29A.56-110 et seq.

Wisconsin – Const. Art. 13, §12; Wis. Stat. Ann. §9.10

Recall is not an easy undertaking and gathering the needed signatures can be a challenge. You should make sure anyone who collects signatures is well educated about the recall and why the official needs to be removed from office. Recall is a very valuable tool when an elected official becomes out of control and abuses their power against the people and Freedom.

******

Chapter 7

Defense against Abusive Law Enforcers & The Lack of Law Enforcement Protecting You From Them.

Because we have given way too much power and authority to Law Enforcers they have become a military power that in many cases runs rogue. Abusing their power has become the norm and they don't care if you like it or not. With local district attorneys and the courts backing them up, they can lie, cheat, steal, and murder without fear. Anyone who questions their authority is routinely bullied and arrested, and there is little you can do about it, or is there?

The Police Chief and Sheriff are most often elected or hired by their cities and counties who are controlled by the City Council and the County Board of Supervisors, who are elected by the people. If you see someone being beat and or arrested by the police just for merely questioning their authority, or your city or county has a known reputation for this happening, then you probably have a Gestapo problem. The Police and Sheriff Deputies hate being called Gestapo, but since the advent of being able to directly upload police and sheriff abuse of power on the internet, the word Gestapo fits. The sad thing is "We The People" have allowed it to get this bad, but not because we weren't warned.

"First they came for the Jews, and I didn't speak out because I wasn't a Jew.

Then they came for the communists, and I didn't speak out because I wasn't a communist.

Then they came for the socialists, and I didn't speak out because I wasn't a socialist.

Then they came for the trade unionists, and I didn't speak out because I wasn't a trade unionist.

Then they came for me, and there was no one left to speak out for me. " – Martin Niemöller

An English translation of Niemöller's speech for the Confessing Church in Frankfurt on the 6th of January 1946 states: "When Pastor Niemöller was put in a concentration camp we wrote the year 1937; when the concentration camp was opened we wrote the year 1933, and the people who were put in the camps then were Communists. Who cared about them? We knew it, it was printed in the newspapers.

Who raised their voice, maybe the Confessing Church? We thought: Communists, those opponents of religion, those enemies of Christians - "should I be my brother's keeper?"

Then they got rid of the sick, the so-called incurables. - I remember a conversation I had with a person who claimed to be a Christian, He said: *"Perhaps it's right, these incurably sick people just cost the state money, they are just a burden to themselves and to others. Isn't it best for all concerned if they are taken out of the middle [of society]?' -- Only then did the church as such take note. Then we started talking, until our voices were again silenced in public. Can we say, we aren't guilty or responsible? The persecution of the Jews, the way we treated the occupied countries, or the things in Greece, in Poland, in Czechoslovakia or in Holland, that were written in the newspapers. I believe, we Confessing-Church-Christians have every reason to say: mea culpa, mea culpa! We can talk ourselves out of it with the excuse that it would have cost me my head if I had spoken out."*

If only people now would stand up and speak out on all of the abusive treatment that has been going on with our people and our country, but ironically most people have the same excuse written above by Martin Niemoller "it might cost me my head". So it seems that history is repeating it self again right here in America. Luckily there are a few of us who are speaking out and denouncing the Gestapo that are infecting our country. But it's going to take a lot more people to change the trend and that means more people speaking out and demanding that this stop.

To do that we have to stand up to our elected officials and demand they put a stop to it, or we will remove them from office, and elect someone else who will put a stop to all the abuse and corruption Only then will we see these rogue bullies be charged with crimes that they committed against the people and hopefully convicted, never to be able to wear a law enforcement uniform ever again. Many of them should have never been allowed to wear one in the first place, from some of the videos that are posted on the internet, but somehow because of who they know, they are allowed to continue their abuse against the taxpaying citizens. A good site to visit is: Flexyourrights.org, there is a lot of good information on that site that you can use to defend yourself from some abusive tactics.

Someone needs to also challenge how search warrants are executed in the US Supreme Court. Gestapo like tactics should not go unchallenged. To allow police to break-down your door and destroy your home, shoot and kill your animals and hold you face-down on the floor while ransacking your home and destroying personal property, should not be tolerated in any free society. Since when was it deemed OK to destroy a citizens personal property just because the government suspects you may have committed a crime? Any law enforcer who tries to lie to you and says they don't destroy personal property needs to be reminded that breaking down a front door is destroying personal property. Police killing a family pet should also be a crime just as killing a police dog is a crime. We the people should never allow ourselves to have less Rights than the police, because if we do, we're living in a police state and that is not Freedom.

State Supreme Courts have condoned and allowed police to do whatever they want whether legal or not, and this cannot be tolerated in a free society. One case in point was in Indianapolis where the state supreme court overturned a common law dating back to the English Magna Carta of 1215, the Indiana Supreme Court ruled in May of 2011 that no one has the right to resist unlawful police entry into their homes.

In a 3-2 decision, Justice Steven David writing for the court said, *"If a police officer wants to enter a home for any reason or no reason at all, a homeowner cannot do anything to block the officer's entry."*

"We believe ... a right to resist an unlawful police entry into a home is against public policy and is incompatible with "modern" Fourth Amendment jurisprudence," David said. *"We also find that allowing resistance unnecessarily escalates the level of violence and therefore the risk of injuries to all parties involved without preventing the arrest."*

David said a person arrested following an unlawful entry by police still can be released on bail and has plenty of opportunities to protest the illegal entry through the court system.

So what he is saying in short, is we have no Rights against Police/Gestapo no matter what they do to you, even kill you. This is a classic case of rewriting the Constitution by inference. Notice the "modern" Fourth Amendment jurisprudence quote and his attempt to cleverly say that resistance is futile because he wasn't going to allow his Gestapo to be put in harms way. This is only one of many cases where our Rights have been overruled by judges that should have never been allowed to sit on any legal bench.

On the flip side of this Law Enforcement equation is the lack of protection by police from the vandals and thieves in this country anymore. Police seem to do little or nothing when we call in to report a theft or vandalization of our property. Yet, if we have a taillight out on our car, watch out, they will pull us over and give us the third degree, probably search our car and then ticket us...and if we question their authority, oh boy, we could be in for a beating and a POP charge.

I have complained several times about the vandalization of my property and the theft of a number of items, only to get smoke blown up my backside by law enforcers who claim they are too busy and/or understaffed. When I asked if an officer could go out and see the vandalization that was done, it took them 5 days to respond. The Vandals destroyed a 1,450 square foot mobile home that I was putting together for my wife and I on the property in Butte County, California that we were hoping one day to eventually live in. They broke every window, shower door, light fixture, mirror, bedroom door, cabinet, and fan, in the place. They also shot holes throughout the home making it a total loss. Since I was in the first stage of the building process, there was no insurance company that would insure me unless I paid thousands, or until I had all of the permits signed. You can not get county permits period until you have HUD sign off on a mobile or modular home in California. You have to have it built before they approve it. So my wife and I ate over $35,000 dollars worth of damage which did not even include the total destruction of a 1966 Kaiser jeep that was parked on the property and a Semi Truck that they broke the windshield and windows out of and slashed two of the tires. They also pushed our boat off of its trailer. It all makes me wonder why we have to pay tax on this property at all! It sure is not for police or sheriff protection against vandals and thieves and they don't even maintain our road and our grown children do not go to the schools. We don't even live up there as planned because of all the damage that has been done! As far as paying tax for fire protection goes, well that is a joke because everything on our property has been trashed so if there was a fire we would have nothing to lose except for maybe the beautiful trees and scenery. But since we do not have the money to start over, we will probably never be able to live there and enjoy that beautiful scenery as planned! I realize that the law enforcers can not be there 24/7. But when you call to report a major vandalism and it takes them 5 days to even come up and look at the damage that is outrageous! Of course by then any evidence that they might have found such as finger prints would be gone and the people that did it will be long gone!!!!

I've come to find out that my horrible story of vandalization is not the exception, but more of the rule. It seems that most everyone that I have spoke with since than, that have property around the same vicinity as mine have had damage done to their property too, and have had pretty much the same results with the law enforcers; which is doing little or nothing to stop the problem. Of course California is not the best place to invest in, so it is partly my fault for attempting to develop my property.

But you would think that our local officials would want their law enforcers to go out and catch the real criminals, not the poor individual who had no idea that their taillight went out on their car. Instead they seem to go after the easy money, while the real hardcore criminals sit around and laugh while getting high on the drugs they bought with the money they made off the things they just stole from you.

I used to think some of the mid-eastern laws were a bit harsh, like if a thief gets caught they cut off a finger, and if they get caught a second time they cut off their hand; but after becoming a victim of vandalism and theft, I am starting to think that law looks pretty good. This is why people have formed Neighborhood Watch Patrols to protect each other against vandals thugs and thieves. The police unfortunately do not seem too interested in going after some of these lowlife criminals. Once again the citizens who live by the rules and obey the laws have become the victims!

So the government imposing laws for our safety is another illusion. Laws are arbitrarily enforced and abused, it is imperative that we take control of our government and return policing back to going after the real criminals, and not a tool for revenue generation and public control.

Here is something to also think about; If a thief or vandal takes or destroys something and is never caught, what do you have to do to replace it?........You have to buy a new one and what do you have to pay extra on what you buy? Bingo.......Taxes! Either income tax, sales tax or both, so once again the revenue generation comes into play. It is all a numbers game to get the masses to make more money and spend more money, and pay more taxes to support the pyramid scheme called "The Government"

****

Chapter 8

Can America Regain It's Freedom?

I will try and be optimistic, so with that I do hope and pray that America will one day be able to get back some of the freedom that it has lost. But unless we all get involved, unfortunately I fear more freedom will be lost. Too many people just do not seem to care. They go along to get along and most people get real uncomfortable when you tell them that they need to get involved. I have shown you some historic facts and figures and some laws to back up my comments, along with the abuse and crimes the government has commit against us. I could go on and on and quote many more cases and facts and show you many other examples, but as I stated at the beginning of this book, my whole effort was to give you some history and facts and try to keep this as short-winded as possible. I hope I was able to accomplish this, and you can now see and understand how unfree we really are. We need to all get off the sidelines and band together and stand up for our rights to help America restore the freedom that was granted under the greatest document ever written!   THE US CONSTITUTION & THE BILL OF RIGHTS

I will leave you with this Statement by Patrick Henry. If you take out all of the reference to the British and the King and replace it with the American Government and President, it fits perfectly today. I just wish that people today would take a stand, as our forefathers did when they stood up against the tyranny and created this nation .

March 23, 1775.

By Patrick Henry

"No man thinks more highly than I do of the patriotism, as well as abilities, of the very worthy gentlemen who have just addressed the house. But different men often see the same subject in different lights; and, therefore, I hope it will not be thought disrespectful to those gentlemen if, entertaining as I do opinions of a character very opposite to theirs, I shall speak forth my sentiments freely and without reserve. This is no time for ceremony. The question before the house is one of awful moment to this country. For my own part, I consider it as nothing less than a question of freedom or slavery; and in proportion to the magnitude of the subject ought to be the freedom of the debate. It is only in this way that we can hope to arrive at the truth, and fulfill the great responsibility which we hold to God and our country. Should I keep back my

opinions at such a time, through fear of giving offense, I should consider myself as guilty of treason towards my country, and of an act of disloyalty toward the Majesty of Heaven, which I revere above all earthly kings.

Mr. President, it is natural to man to indulge in the illusions of hope. We are apt to shut our eyes against a painful truth, and listen to the song of that siren till she transforms us into beasts. Is this the part of wise men, engaged in a great and arduous struggle for liberty? Are we disposed to be of the numbers of those who, having eyes, see not, and, having ears, hear not, the things which so nearly concern their temporal salvation? For my part, whatever anguish of spirit it may cost, I am willing to know the whole truth, to know the worst, and to provide for it.

I have but one lamp by which my feet are guided, and that is the lamp of experience. I know of no way of judging of the future but by the past. And judging by the past, I wish to know what there has been in the conduct of the British ministry for the last ten years to justify those hopes with which gentlemen have been pleased to solace themselves and the House. Is it that insidious smile with which our petition has been lately received?

Trust it not, sir; it will prove a snare to your feet. Suffer not yourselves to be betrayed with a kiss. Ask yourselves how this gracious reception of our petition comports with those warlike preparations which cover our waters and darken our land. Are fleets and armies necessary to a work of love and reconciliation? Have we shown ourselves so unwilling to be reconciled that force must be called in to win back our love? Let us not deceive ourselves, sir. These are the implements of war and subjugation; the last arguments to which Kings resort. I ask gentlemen, sir, what means this martial array, if its purpose be not to force us to submission? Can gentlemen assign any other possible motive for it? Has Great Britain any enemy, in this quarter of the world, to call for all this accumulation of navies and armies? No, sir, she has none. They are meant for us: they can be meant for no other. They are sent over to bind and rivet upon us those chains which the British ministry have been so long forging. And what have we to oppose to them? Shall we try argument? Sir, we have been trying that for the last ten years. Have we anything new to offer upon the subject? Nothing! We have held the subject up in every light of which it is capable; but it has been all in vain. Shall we resort to entreaty and humble supplication? What terms shall we find which have not been already exhausted?

Let us not, I beseech you, sir, deceive ourselves. Sir, we have done everything that could be done to avert the storm which is now coming on. We have petitioned; we have remonstrated; we have supplicated; we have prostrated ourselves before the throne, and have implored its interposition to arrest the tyrannical hands of the ministry and Parliament. Our petitions have been slighted; our remonstrances have produced additional violence and insult; our supplications have been disregarded; and we have been spurned, with contempt, from the foot of the throne! In vain, after these things, may we indulge the fond hope of peace and reconciliation.

There is no longer any room for hope. If we wish to be free-- if we mean to preserve inviolate those inestimable privileges for which we have been so long contending--if we mean not basely to abandon the noble struggle in which we have been so long engaged, and which we have pledged ourselves never to abandon until the glorious object of our contest shall be obtained--we must fight! I repeat it, sir, we must fight! An appeal to arms and to the God of hosts is all that is left us! They tell us, sir, that we are weak; unable to cope with so formidable an adversary. But when shall we be stronger? Will it be the next week, or the next year? Will it be when we are totally disarmed, and when a British guard shall be stationed in every house? Shall we gather strength by irresolution and inaction? Shall we acquire the means of effectual resistance by lying supinely on our backs and hugging the delusive phantom of hope, until our enemies shall have bound us hand and foot? Sir, we are not weak if we make a proper use of those means which the God of nature hath placed in our power. The millions of people, armed in the holy cause of liberty, and in such a country as that which we possess, are invincible by any force which our enemy can send against us. Besides, sir, we shall not fight our battles alone. There is a just God who presides over the destinies of nations, and who will raise up friends to fight our battles for us. The battle, sir, is not to the strong alone; it is to the vigilant, the active, the brave. Besides, sir, we have no election. If we were base enough to desire it, it is now too late to retire from the contest. There is no retreat but in submission and slavery! Our chains are forged! Their clanking may be heard on the plains of Boston! The war is inevitable--and let it come! I repeat it, sir, let it come.

It is in vain, sir, to extentuate the matter. Gentlemen may cry, Peace, Peace--but there is no peace. The war is actually begun! The next gale that sweeps from the north will bring to our ears the clash of resounding arms! Our brethren are already in the field! Why stand we here idle? What is it that gentlemen wish? What would they have? Is life so dear, or peace so sweet, as to be purchased at the price of chains and slavery? Forbid it, Almighty God! I know not what course others may take; but as for me, give me liberty or give me death!"

I hope that now you have finished reading this book it has given you some knowledge and encouragement to become more politically involved! The choice is up to you. Will it be: Freedom or Enslavement? America is running out of time and our freedom depends on each and everyone of you to help us survive!

****

Notes:

Special Thanks to my wife; S.E. Gless for her editing.

Credits

Some of the information in this book was gathered from: The Early Years of American Law - Colonial Freedom, Britain's Push For Greater Control, A New Start, A New Criminal Court System - JRank Articles http://law.jrank.org/pages/11900/Early-Years-American-Law.html#ixzz2bgK18tXY. Wikipedia.org and Pictures taken by RW Gless.

www.ingramcontent.com/pod-product-compliance
Lightning Source LLC
Chambersburg PA
CBHW070912290526
45795CB00001B/290